I AM JON
Born to Be Me

by
DAMIAN CHANDLER

Watersprings
PUBLISHING

Published by Watersprings Publishing a division of Watersprings Media House, LLC.
P.O. BOX 1284
Olive Branch, MS 38654
www.waterspringsmedia.com
Contact publisher for bulk orders and permission requests.

Copyrights © 2019 by Damian Chandler. All rights reserved.

No part of this publication may be reproduced, distributed, or transmitted in any form or by any means, including photocopying, recording, or other electronic or mechanical methods, without the prior written permission of the publisher, except in the case of brief quotations embodied in critical reviews and certain other non-commercial uses permitted by copyright law.

Scripture taken from The Message. Copyright © 1993, 1994, 1995, 1996, 2000, 2001, 2002. Used by permission of NavPress Publishing Group.

Cover Illustrator: Cameron T. Wilson

Printed in the United States of America.

ISBN-13: 978-1-948877-33-6

I AM JON

Born to Be Me

No Weapons

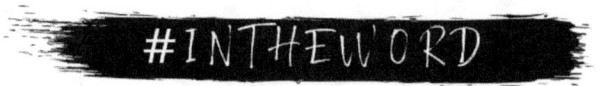

1 SAMUEL 13

19-20 *There wasn't a blacksmith to be found anywhere in Israel. The Philistines made sure of that—"Lest those Hebrews start making swords and spears." That meant that the Israelites had to go down among the Philistines to keep their tools sharp and in good repair.*

22 *So when the battle of Micmash was joined, there wasn't a sword or spear to be found anywhere in Israel—except for Saul and his son Jonathan; they were both well-armed.*

Chapter 1

NO WEAPONS

Funny what you can know if you just open your eyes and listen.

    I had learned to look out of the kitchen window and watch for the way dad drove into the driveway. The easy emergence of lights peacefully crawling into the kitchen, with a smooth turn and gentle stop meant all was well. It was a good day. But when lights screamed, and the turn was sudden and jerky as though he thought about passing the driveway all together, and the stop was coupled with an angry screech inches before crashing through that same window, I knew all hell had broken loose. And if I didn't hurry up and get out of the kitchen, a bad day for him would become a bad day for me. So, I would grab my stuff, run to my room and shut the door. Never even turning on the lights.

    But he had been having a lot of those days recently, and today, I was just too tired to run. So, I just sat there at that small table in the kitchen and braced myself for the tornado about to blast through the door.

No Weapons

Car lights turned off. Car door slammed. He was angry. Kitchen door swung open so fast it looked as though it was just trying to get out of his way. He walked in, threw his bag to the floor and just stood there, staring at it.

I wasn't sure if I was supposed to talk, but saying nothing felt even more uncomfortable.

"Hey dad!"

No answer. He walked over to the fridge and opened it, and as quickly he slammed it shut as if his appetite had suddenly disappeared. Now he was pacing.

"Dad what's wrong?"

"I knew it! I knew it!" He was talking, and I happened to be in the room, but he was not talking to me. "Another one gone. Caleb is transferring!"

My heart sank.

From the moment we heard that the city had voted for that new gym, we knew they were trying to sink us. Coastal Valley's new campus was going to be bad for our school and our team. We had always been the underdogs, always under-sourced. Wrong zip code, I guess. But now, the gap between us and them was wider than the Black Hole. This did not tip the scale. It smashed it. What parent wanted their kid to come to a school where the computers were broken, air conditioners forgotten, and even the porta potties were out of order. Our stuff was so old that on the first day of school last year, Lucy Faulkner sat at her desk, opened the lid, and saw

I Am Jon

her father's name scribbled on the inside. Her father hadn't attended our school in over 30 years.

So no one blamed the parents who moved their kids, but still, it hurt. It hurt deep. Best friends were separated, relationships broken up. But by far, the deepest wound was inflicted by Mrs. Smith, one of our own teachers. She did the unthinkable. She transferred her daughter to Coastal, said it was because of some science program or something they had over there. But the shame that covered her face as she walked the hallways told us all that her reason was a lot less than true.

Honestly, I think we all understood that feeling of shame. It covered our faces too. It was felt whenever they called our school "The Jungle" because of the knee high, uncut grass. It was felt whenever they called our school a jail because of the bars that covered the broken first-floor windows. Shame. Shame and abandonment.

The city obviously didn't care. They had long given up on us. And now, students were doing the same. Without even waving a goodbye or whispering a thank you, they walked away. Truth be told, some ran. And left staring out of those broken and barred windows were a bunch of kids not bold enough to follow them out the door.

So, though we understood their reasons for leaving, seeing the empty desks of close friends hurt. And it hurt our team badly.

After the gym was opened, the city decided to

No Weapons

have the summer basketball league there. They wanted to give all the kids in the area a peek at their new toy. It was the biggest advertising campaign Coastal could have gotten, and they definitely played it up. Tours of their locker rooms. Refreshments in their player lounge. I hear they even showed one top recruit what it would look like to see his name on their big, new, digital score board. Whatever you could think of, they had more of. Whatever we had, they had better.

    Half our team spent the entire summer in that gym. They had no choice. It was the only one open. So, we lost a lot of players. Our best weapons. And for the ones that actually came back, they walked into our old gym with a dark cloud hanging over them. The whole team spent warmups talking about how great Coastal's new place was and how great their team was going to be. "Y'all see that floor?"

    "I walked in and was like..."

    "Those locker rooms tho."

    "Dope."

    "Flat screens everywhere."

    "Hot tub y'all. They got a hot tub."

    Laughter. Agreement. Pause.

    "Forget all that stuff. None of that matters," Dan voiced. Dan's face wore his worry as he said, "I was there one-night and five dudes walked in. Their players. They showed up for a pickup game. They were giants. Every single one of them. Even the point guard had to be 6'6"."

Dan. He was prone to stretching the truth by more than an inch. But this time he wasn't far off—I knew for a fact that that point guard Billy Newsome was a legit 6'4" and he was the shortest guy in their starting 5." The tallest guy on our team, was Ben and he was only 6'5". "They were unbeatable. Ran grown men off the court. Grown men! They ran through every team twice…and then walked off the floor. It was unbelievable!"

The silence of that moment was loud. The dark cloud over the gym grew darker and hung low. It felt as though even before the first whistle had blown, we were already defeated. I had to snatch them back. "If I had not known better, I would say that you boys sound scared. I thought this was warmup. Sounds like a pity party. Keep your minds on what we are doing here. Anybody who wants to spend all their time talking about Coastal, needs to just change squads and go run with them. But in here, we are focused on us. Quad stretch. Let's go!"

What I had said was dangerous. Truth was, every player in that gym would have left just to sit on Coastal's bench. Good thing they only had fifteen spots.

I think I happened to be in that gym that night too. I couldn't tell the team that. They would never understand. But something in me said that I needed to get it out of my system, had to see it at least once before we had to play them there, or I might spend the whole game distracted by their new stuff. I wanted to go on a night when I knew it was going to be packed, so I could at least lose myself in the crowd. Thinking about that now, it doesn't make sense. But I didn't want anyone to see me in that place. Didn't want to have to answer questions.

It was exactly what everyone said it was. What the city had said it would be.

"Mr. Mayor can you tell us, why build this gym? Why now?"

"This is for our children. We need to make an investment now for every future generation." Canned answer. Fake smile. Flashing camera. I had heard dad talking about it. I knew that this had nothing to do with youth or any future generation. It was about Mayor John Saber. He needed something big to make people forget all of the stories floating around Dyer. Favors that were given. Monies that had disappeared. He wanted a monument, a memorial that would forever bare his name.

Few wanted to be tied to that name. Many had the integrity to say no. But not Coastal. They saw opportunity and didn't mind his monument being built on their campus as long as it provided them with a new gym. At their school board meeting, someone made a motion to name the gym in his honor. There wasn't even a single "no" vote. Coastal's gym would be called Saber Gymnasium.

Mayor Saber graciously accepted, then proceeded to reroute money from every city project to his new jewel—every project, including the renovation of our gym. We had stood in line waiting our turn for over a decade, always pushed to the back, always something more important, always delayed. A bunch of us students even went to the city council meeting. I read our letter.

"This is why we need your help." Applause.

The Mayor paused and gave a camera ready smile stating, "We are so proud to see our young people exercising their civil rights today. The youth of today are the leaders of tomorrow. Our city is in good hands." Blah. Blah. Blah. " But…"

And then every member of that counsel proceeded to explain that it was irresponsible for a small city like ours to take on more than one major project. And fixing our school was just not as important as repairing the water main or fixing the Mill Creek Bridge. Then, they all came down from their perches on podiums, hunting for microphones and photo ops.

"You kids did so good. Maybe one day you'll be the ones to sit up there in those seats. Remember, if you set your sights on the stars, you'll at least reach the sun." Fake smile. Camera. Flash.

But then the announcement of this gym. All that "irresponsible" talk was tossed in the garbage quicker than an old newspaper. Water mains and broken bridges were all forgotten. And all the money in the city was rerouted to building Coastal a gym.

So as I walked those halls and stood in the corner of that gym, I steamed. Because they took money

No Weapons

meant to fix our broken windows and threw it into construction of their glass walls. Money to renovate our condemned science building paid for retractable bleachers and a smoothie bar. Our art and music programs were cut, but they got sculptures in their halls and a grand piano in their lobby. I saw the hot tub in the locker room too.

Lies. The more I saw, the louder my mind screamed. Lies. They just lied. I had always known they were lying but walking the halls of their lie was maddening. I felt sick. Wanted to puke. And I knew that was exactly the feeling of every player sitting in our half-lit dungeon. But I had to lead, and I couldn't let them know how I felt. Not now. Maybe not ever.

The guys all fell silent and got into the quad stretch. Dan got up and walked over to the only water fountain in our gym to take a sip before we threw ourselves into practice. Like everything else, it didn't work. He exploded, "The only water fountain in this entire gym ain't working. It never works! Hasn't worked properly since I was a freshman. They can get a waterfall in the lobby, but we can't get one working water fountain? *That's not fair!*" Dan kicked the fountain so hard the front panel dropped off.

He was right. It wasn't fair. They had everything. Way beyond everything. We had nothing. Less than nothing. And they would do everything in their power to keep it that way.

Our last boast-worthy hope was Caleb Williams, our starting forward. We all knew that of all the things they could say, they could never say they had Caleb. And that was a big deal. He and his family had long ties to our school. At one point, I think his grandfather was a teacher there, his mom subbed for the school secretary, and his dad was head of our booster club. They were Providence High.

And Caleb? He was one of the best players in the state. From the time he was a sophomore, we had seen coaches from college programs trickling into our gym like mice to cheese. We always knew who they were there to see. But secretly, every other player in that gym clung to the fleeting hope that he could show those coaches his worth. Never worked. They would all watch Caleb all the way through practice, talk to my dad about him after, and leave, never once glancing at the rest of us. It was as if, for them, the rest of us were just necessary props for someone else's audition. And who could blame them. Caleb was just one of those guys. He was born with "it", an indescribable gift. When you saw him on a basketball court, you knew that he was doing what he was born to do.

We all saw it. We all knew. Caleb's game was on another level and none of us were even close. But strangely we weren't mad about it. There wasn't even a strain of hate in our hearts toward him. With him there couldn't be. He was such a nice guy. A humble guy. He never acted like the he was the best player on the team. In fact, if he knew how good he was, he never let on to it. He just loved being a part of our team. One of the guys. And though we all knew he wasn't just "one of the guys", we were happy to treat him that way.

But now they had him too. Caleb was transferring. Followed the advice of recruiters from big time universities who wanted to see him perform on a bigger stage.

"Dad how can they do this? He doesn't even live in that district!"

"They just used the address of a "relative" on the other side like everybody else."

"I never thought he would leave. He said he was staying."

"People say stuff they don't mean son."

"Caleb promised."

"Well what did you expect Jon? You thought he was just gonna stick around cause y'all made some pact? A pinky promise? You thought he was going to stay just cause you called him your best friend or something?"

I was silent.

"It doesn't work that way boy. Life doesn't work that way. No one wants to wear our 4-year-old uniforms, climb the rafters to hang buckets to catch the leaks, try to get water from a fountain that don't work, sweat to death in the summer with no air-conditioning or freeze cause the furnace broke." Then he screamed, "No one is loyal Jon. So don't expect them to stay. Don't you ever expect them to stay." He paused and caught himself, "Sorry."

"That's ok."

It wasn't ok. But I had gotten used to it, immune to the screams. But the message stuck. "They are not loyal." "They don't stay." "They don't keep their promises." I could never allow my heart to grow that cold, that dark. No matter how things looked, I had a hope and I would never let it go. "Well, what are we gonna do?"

"We are just gonna have to find a way to use what we got son! We got you, and we got me. And we ain't going nowhere."

He smiled. But his smile was painful, and the pain was honest. What he had said was at least half true. We had each other. Yes. But I would not believe that we were all we had. We were for sure in the fire, and I had heard some pastor preach that when you are in the fire, you are never there alone. I believed that then. And I believe it still.

1 SAMUEL 14

2-3 *Meanwhile, Saul was taking it easy under the pomegranate tree at the threshing floor on the edge of town at Geba. There were about six hundred men with him. Ahijah, wearing the priestly Ephod, was also there. But no one there knew that Jonathan had gone off.*

1 SAMUEL 14

1 *Later that day, Jonathan, Saul's son, said to his armor bearer, "Come on, let's go over to the Philistine garrison patrol on the other side of the pass." But he didn't tell his father.*

4-7 *He said to his armor bearer, "Come on now, let's go across to these uncircumcised pagans. Maybe God will work for us. There's no rule that says God can only deliver by using a big army. No one can stop God from saving when he sets his mind to it." His armor bearer said, "Go ahead. Do what you think best. I'm with you all the way."*

Chapter 2

NO MORE MEETINGS

I stood at the line in the empty gym shooting free throws. Don't even know how many I had shot. 50? 100? 200? I had lost count. Time and shots seemed to fly by when I was in that gym alone. And I was alone in there a lot. Dad had the keys, and I knew where he kept them. So many evenings I would ride 3 blocks, past the park, past the corner store, hopped the fence, unlocked the chain on the door and stood at the free throw line alone. Sometimes I came to practice. Other times I came to escape. Either way, that gym had become a place I ran to when I needed to get away.

But on this day, I was not quite alone. The gym could not shelter me from the stress I was trying to escape. Dad had a meeting with the other coaches and the principal in the far corner office of the gym, and when the principal was present, that was never a good sign. Dad was in trouble.

The door was solid... closed. But the glass window was paper thin. I could see dad. He was pacing. The principal was screaming. This meeting wasn't

No More Meetings

going well.

"Coach the team is losing. And the boosters are talking."

"What do you mean we're losing? We're 5-4!" Dad's frustration was bubbling.

"Morale around here is at an all-time low."

"I know."

"People are not coming to the games anymore, and that is becoming a big problem."

"Are you planning to tell me something I don't know Mr. Principal."

"Yeah. Try this. I stuck my neck out to hire you, son. And people are talking, saying that you are in way over your head. Had a group of parents in my office this week demanding that you be fired. Now, I've decided to be gracious coach, extend a little mercy. But grace and mercy can only go so far. High school ball is big business now, and we want what all the other big programs got, facilities, recognition. We want people talking about Providence again. This city needs it. We deserve it. So do what we brought you here to do, or I will have to find someone else who can. Beat Coastal!"

That's all it was about. Coastal Valley. The same Coastal Valley that had beat us 3 years in a row now, whose board had convinced the city to re-route money meant for other schools including Providence to build them that brand new campus. They lured all the talent and teachers in town with their big campus and high-tech gym, leaving our school with no players and no resources. We kept losing to them. And there was nothing to make us think that this year was going to be any different. The losing was frustrating. Embarrassing. It's not like we hadn't won any games. But even when we were winning it felt like we were losing because all people talked about was Coastal. I had made the team as a freshman (everybody said it was because my dad was the coach, but I outworked every other player on the court and proved them wrong). Still, not one win against them. Not one! And it didn't seem as though that was about to change. It stuck in my craw like popcorn in my teeth. I couldn't ignore it. I couldn't shake it. I desperately wanted to beat them too.

So sometimes, I just "happened" to be in the office when the coaches met. And I itched to share my plan of how to beat the Giants. I thought about it all the time. I had drawn plays and all. They tolerated my interruptions with smiles. But I soon realized their smiles were not an invitation to the table. These were soaked in a sarcasm that my senses missed. And so they nodded yes to everything I said and then moved past as if I had said nothing at all. And for the rest of the meeting, it was as if I were not there. By the time dad showed up at the next practice, it was clear that he had not listened. He never did. He came to practice with the same old plan, same old plays. And every year, same result.

After a while, I stopped going to their meetings.

As far as I was concerned, nothing came of their meetings anyway. Sometimes adults talk and talk, and continue to talk so that no one ever notices that they don't know what to do.

So I stopped talking. Talking made no difference. But inside, I burned.

NOT SO ALONE

Two hours later, dad came out of that meeting. He looked like he had been body-slammed in a fight, so defeated he couldn't even lift his head. I hated seeing him this way. But I had seen him that way a lot lately. As he walked by, he mumbled something in my direction. I assumed he'd said, "See you at home" because he just left.

I heard the outer door of the gym slam. Everyone had left now, and I was finally alone. And in the dim, half-lit gym, I did what I always did when I was alone there. I imagined the day we beat Coastal Valley. And it was always with a last second shot, by me. Get the pass. Cross over. Jab step. Fade away. Ball leaves hands. Perfect form. Perfect rotation. Nothing but net. Funny how no one ever misses imaginary shots. The echo of the ball bouncing on the floor was the sound of raucous applause as I ran around the gym, mobbed by my teammates, high-fiving the fans in the expensive court-side seats.

"Providence Wins! Providence Wins! Providence Wins!"

I Am Jon

"Not so sure about that. Their 7-footer would have swatted your flat shot into Never Never Land!" I lost all the bass in my voice and struggled not to release my liquids. Didn't know there was anyone else in the gym. I looked in the direction of the voice. It was dark over there.

My eyes slowly adjusting, "Who is that?"

"Who did you expect dork? Its Michal."

"I keep telling you, stop calling me Dork."

My best friend—no person on the planet outside of my parents, that I had known longer. Including my parents, no one I had talked to more. And, till I hit my 11-year-old Thank-You-Jesus growth spurt, there was no one who murdered me on the basketball court like her. She was quick, smart, with a devastating crossover and smooth jumper. I loved to watch her embarrass boys who thought girls can't hoop. Fact, we used to run game at the park where she showed up at a court, acting like she couldn't play and then toasted boys while their friends watched. I caught a few of those on video. Got more than a few IG hits.

"You need to stop doing that! I almost..."

"Calm down. The door was open, and the lights were on, so I knew you were in here. Plus that game is this week, so I figured you were getting up some shots."

"I'm just tired of losing to them Michal. Tired of the smug looks on their faces. Tired of hearing, 'Maybe next time'. Tired of having to tell Stan that it

No More Meetings

was close."

"Stan? Who's Stan?"

"That guy who works the produce section at the grocery store. He only seems to ask about games after we lose. When we win, I can never find him."

"Maybe this is your year. I'm sure your dad has a plan."

She had much more confidence in dad's plans than I did. He had been our peewee league coach, had introduced her to the game. So she still had a soft spot for him.

"Same plan he had last year. And the year before that. And the year before that. They meet and talk and plan, and then, we go out on the court and get slaughtered. I'm tired of all the talk. I want to win. And I know how we can!"

I can't tell you how many times we had done this. We would sit on her front porch and strategize how we could beat some older boys at ball. I was always the decoy; she always had the last shot. So this kind of talk was not new. It's what we did. So it felt natural to share my plan with her. I knew she would always listen. I talked about every player— their strengths and their weaknesses, whether they drove to their left or their right. I knew it all.

"I guess you are the son of a coach," said Michal.

I ignored her comment and now I was pacing like dad had been.

"They don't think we can beat them. They don't think we can win. But that is exactly how we beat them."

"Thank God! At least I agree with them on one thing. Neither of us thinks you can win," Michal teased.

"We got to beat them from the post. From the inside."

"That will never work with those behemoths they got over there."

"Yeah they are bigger. And I'll even admit that they are stronger. But we are faster, and we want it more!"

"Jon that is not our strength. We are shooters."

"That is exactly my point. They expect us to come out, milk the clock, try to keep it close and run those dinosaur plays. We have to do something new, try something different. We run. We press. And then we pound it inside. Beat them at their own game."

"They will never expect that a team as small as yours would attack them inside the key. No one does."

"Yup they would never expect it! And when they finally defend it, we launch from the outside and we keep launching."

"That is the stupidest plan I have ever heard." She was right. It was a stupid plan and I knew it. No basketball guru would ever approve of it. Most people would laugh at it. And at one time, fear of their laughter would have been enough to keep me silent. But any fear I had once felt in sharing my idea was long gone. I realized that every once in a while, a good, stupid plan is exactly what we need.

"Listen. We've tried everything else, and nothing has worked. Why not try something different? This could work!"

"It really could work. Why don't you tell your dad?"

"He doesn't listen to me. He never has. But we could make it work!"

"Well...nothing else in 3 years has worked and this plan is as good as anything else you guys got. You got my vote. Now, if it doesn't work, you know I'm gonna clown you right?" We laughed.

"You wouldn't be you if you didn't...Really wish you were out there with me."

"I am. Every time you play, I'm there with you. You can't get rid of me."

My soul knew that what she was saying was true. She was always with me.

That night, we talked a little more as I walked her home. I got back to the house later than usual, but dad was still up, still looking hopeless. Defeated. He looked my way... I was about to tell him about what Michal, and I had talked about at the gym, but before words left my mouth, I snatched them back. Decided to say nothing at all.

I Am Jon

1 SAMUEL 8
4-5 *Fed up, all the elders of Israel got together and confronted Samuel. They presented their case: "Look, you're an old man, and your sons aren't following in your footsteps. Here's what we want you to do: Appoint a king to rule us, just like everybody else."*

1 SAMUEL 9
1-2 *There was a man from the tribe of Benjamin named Kish. He had a son, Saul, a most handsome young man. There was none finer—he literally stood head and shoulders above the crowd!*

1 SAMUEL 10:21b-22
21b *But when they went looking for him, he was nowhere to be found.*
22 *Samuel went back to God: "Is he anywhere around?" God said, "Yes, he's right over there—hidden in that pile of baggage."*

Chapter 3

WE WANT A COACH

I sometimes feel the need to defend my dad. Often, really. The coach that I hear people talking about, gossiping about in school halls and grocery aisles, is just not the man I know. For them, what he does on the court is who he is. From their safe seats in bleachers, I hear them criticizing every substitution, trashing every play as if the plays they call in their own lives are any better. And then they go from criticizing his coaching to criticizing him. But Dad taught me to ignore it.

"If you're gonna live in the spotlight son, expect to get burned." "Jon remember: the leader always gets the most lashes." "No matter what they do, we will never allow ourselves to sink to their level."

Sounds good. But it didn't help. My insides just couldn't ignore it. They still screamed. Sometimes things I am not at all that proud of. So whenever I needed to let off steam, Michal met me at the park and just let me vent.

"He's not who they say he is. They don't even know him."

"I know."

"They don't know how hard he worked. How much he cares about this team. If they knew him, they would love him like I love him."

"But they don't, and they won't." Obviously she was in one of her matter of fact moods.

"You know, sometimes I wish he'd just quit. He never wanted the job in the first place. He never asked for it. And sometimes I wish he never took it."

"Jon you really don't mean that."

But it was true. And sometimes I did mean it. On those days, these were not thoughtless words from a careless kid. I had thought about how our lives would have been different if he weren't Coach. Not sure that I would have been playing high school ball, but really, that would have been a small sacrifice to get back what we had lost. And we had lost a lot.

Before basketball, we were simple people from a respectable family. Pops owned the most popular mechanic shop in town, Jacobs Brothers Auto Repair. My dad and his two brothers were born with their heads under car hoods, and there was no doubt in anybody's mind that they were sure to die there.

Then one summer, dad had a 3-inch growth spurt, and he went from a scrawny 7th grader to a 6 foot 8th grader. And then another jump, and he was a 6'3" freshman. Coaches of every sport circled like vultures over day-old roadkill.

"He was born to be a football player."

"He's a born pitcher."

We Want A Coach

"With a body like that he should be a sprinter."

Wrestler, hockey player, lacrosse. Some guy even told Pop that he should think about getting into water polo. Dad had never been in a pool. Everybody had their own idea of what dad was supposed to be. And they all thought their idea was right.

But Pop was a man of faith and he told dad, "The Good Lord gave you a gift, son, and only He knows what it's for. So when He is good and ready, He will tell you, and then you will know." Wisdom.

And he did. The first day dad touched a basketball, he knew what his gift was for and so did everyone else. Didn't start pretty, that was for sure. He had talent, but that talent was blood-red raw. But he loved the sport and was willing to put in the work to be good at it. So while his brothers honed their skills on cars and carburetors, he lived his life on the basketball court. All that work paid off. He made the Providence varsity team as a sophomore.

Now basketball in Dyer was a lot different then. First of all, our little town was boring and sleepy. But no matter how boring things got, we always had basketball season. It was the one thing everybody in town looked forward to. It was the place where we gathered and met. Everything happened around the court. It was simpler then.

"Dad said the fans used to spray paint their hair like they'd seen fans on TV do and everybody met at 12 points before the game."

"Yeah. Home games were rocking. People even

went to away games too," Michal said.

"They would all meet at the school and we would drive down together, hazard lights flashing the whole 10 miles to Stillwater or 13 miles to Walnut Creek."

"Those were great days."

By the beginning of his senior year my dad was one of the best in the county. He led Providence to their first division 4 state finals.

"People still talk about that team to this day," I said picking up a stone and mindlessly throwing it into the tall grass across the street. "And that was what, 30 years ago?"

"Yup. I was at the barbershop and some older guys were debating whether that team could have won state!" Michal rolled her eyes. We had all heard this argument a million times before. The story had become a legend greater than Sasquatch.

"If "Big" Tom Miller hadn't fouled out…"

"Well, why did he foul out? It was that ref. I'm telling you he had it in for us. You know he was one of those Walker boys, right? And where'd they graduate from, huh? Ferndale!"

And so the conspiracy grew. They lost that year to Ferndale High, but dad moved on and became the first player from our school recruited to a big-time college program. He was the first player from our school recruited to any program.

He stayed away for two years and then returned home. Said something about missing Dyer, but that had never made much sense, that is, until my uncles

We Want A Coach

told me he actually came home because he didn't make the cut. He walked off of the court and back into Pops shop and had no intentions of looking back.

Years passed and things changed. People changed. The magic of TV exposed our little town to big city life. And the more they saw of big city living, the more they wanted big city living in Dyer. All of a sudden, everything that was, was not enough. Everything, including Providence basketball.

"We've got to stop thinking so small. We gotta dream big."

"We need to have a big-time program."

"All the other schools got it. We want it too."

And all big-time programs needed a big-time coach, one who knew the game, had the experience— a winning pedigree. The only person remotely like that in town was dad. That's when the boosters came calling.

"It's time for you to give back to our community."

"Your school needs you."

"Think about the kids."

All their foolery didn't trick dad. He knew this had nothing to do with community or school or kids. Their greed stunk like rotten eggs, and dad wanted nothing to do with it. But he decided to ask Pops what he thought.

"Well son, the Good Lord gave you a gift. Whenever He gives you a gift, He expects you to use it."

"But Pop, I don't want this. I'm done with

basketball."

"Why? Cause you are afraid to fail? You can only fail if you don't try son."

Dad finally did say yes. Then they wanted a press conference. For the kids of course. You know, "Like the big cities do!"

Dad was not that guy. The day of the press conference dad went to the shop and did what he had always done. Opened the hood of a car and stuck his head in it. He never did show up to the press conference and left the principal to answer all the questions So the one reporter from the one newspaper asked the principal what the goal for the team was, and he said, "Beat Coastal Valley!" So that was the mission from the very first day.

Thirty

1 SAM 14

24-27 Saul did something really foolish. He addressed the army: "A curse on the man who eats anything before evening, before I've wreaked vengeance on my enemies!" None of them ate a thing all day. There were honeycombs here and there in the fields. But no one so much as put his finger in the honey to taste it, for the soldiers to a man feared the curse.

1 SAMUEL 14

27-29 But Jonathan hadn't heard his father put the army under oath. He stuck the tip of his staff into some honey and ate it. Refreshed, his eyes lit up with renewed vigor. A soldier spoke up, "Your father has put the army under solemn oath, saying, 'A curse on the man who eats anything before evening!' No wonder the soldiers are drooping!" Jonathan said, "My father has imperiled the country."

1 SAMUEL 14

38-39 Saul then said, "All army officers, step forward. Some sin has been committed this day. We're going to find out what it is and who did it! As God lives, Israel's Savior God, whoever sinned will die, even if it should turn out to be Jonathan, my son!" Nobody said a word.

43-45 Saul confronted Jonathan. "What did you do? Tell me!" Jonathan said, "I licked a bit of honey off the tip of the staff I was carrying. That's it—and for that I'm to die?". The soldiers rose up: "Jonathan—die? Never! He's just carried out this stunning salvation victory for Israel. As surely as God lives, not a hair on his head is going to be harmed. Why, he's been working hand-in-hand with God all day!" The soldiers rescued Jonathan and he didn't die.

Chapter 4

THIRTY

As days passed, the atmosphere at the house became increasingly uncomfortable. There is tension that you can cut with a knife, and then there is tension that snaps knives like twigs. What we were experiencing at home was the latter, and that monster stalked us from our house to the school. Dad would drop me off at the drop-off line and then drive over to the teacher's parking lot and sit in his car until the bell rung, coming in at the last possible moment. That was not like him.

And who could blame him? What had been whispers around the halls and in the locker, room was now a full-blown roar. His job was at stake. Everyone was talking about it. Everyone had an opinion. I imagine he just got tired of talking about it. The fact was we had to win. But nothing on paper said winning was possible. That hopelessness followed him everywhere like a shadow. Everywhere, including our practices.

Now no one would have ever accused my dad of being an easygoing coach. His saying was "You ain't

Thirty

practiced till you felt it." And he made sure we "felt it" every day. But somehow, we had fun doing it, and by the end of the practice, we limped and laughed our way to the locker rooms. Then, he would come walking in and tell some corny joke as if that would heal our wounds.

But as his stress levels rose, so did the intensity of our practices, and fun left the building. He had forgotten that we were not just a team. We were family. He forgot how to inspire us, and so, all he had left were threats and scare tactics...and fear.

"Can someone tell me the score of the last game?"

"I don't know Coach, but what I do know is that we beat those boys so bad somebody should have called an ambulance." That was Leland. We called him Lee because he hated his name. He was forever the comedian of the team. But I sensed that this was not the time for jokes.

"Score?"

"52-40" I finally said.

"52-40. We beat them by twelve points. Twelve points! A team that no one expects to even make regionals." He was already screaming. "A team that has only won three league games so far, and one of them was by forfeit, and we only beat them by twelve? Twelve? Does anybody know how much Coastal beat them by? Thirty! Thirty points! How do we expect to beat Coastal when you can barely beat a team of nobodies! Do you know why we only won by 12? Because *you* missed 10 free throws. So here is what we are going to do. Today you guys are going to go to that free-throw line as a team and shoot thirty straight free throws as a team. Thirty straight! No misses! Every time you miss, you start over. And no one gets water until you are done!"

Thirty straight? When it came to free throws, Ben our center was illiterate. He couldn't hit a free throw if a free throw hit him. There was no way we could get to thirty with him shooting. "We can give you thirty with Ben out." Dan suggested.

"You will give me thirty with Ben in! And not a sip until you do. On the line!" With that, he marched off the court to his office and slammed the door.

What dad had asked for was impossible. Unreasonable.The whole team knew it, but we walked to the line. Everyone standing on the key. Everyone taking their time. First shot up. First shot good. Second shot up. The same. Maybe we can do this. Maybe it is not as impossible as it seemed. "Come on boys we got this."

It would continue that way till it reached Ben. We cheered him on. We encouraged him. He missed it! "That's all right Ben...we got this."

Second round. Same result. Third round. Same. By the fifth round, some of the good shooters started to miss their shots. Ninth round. Tenth round. Fifteen. Eighteen. Twenty rounds. And in all those rounds, Ben had managed to hit two free throws just once. There

Thirty

was no way he was gonna score 3 times in a row. I could tell he felt bad. But it wasn't really his fault.

"Sorry guys."

"It's cool Ben. You'll get it this time."

He was never going to get it. He knew it. We all knew it. I looked over to the busted thermometer in the corner. It read 90 degrees. There was no air-conditioning in our gym and the windows hadn't been opened in years. The only relief to the abuse of heat was one door on the opposite side of the gym. It was a literal hell. Sweat dripped from our faces and exploded on the floor. Most of us were hunched over, hands on our knees. We were exhausted. Defeated!

"This is ridiculous! You would think we lost or something. We are being punished for a game we won! I'm done." I started to walk over toward the water cooler. Every member of the team stopped. They watched.

Izzie tried to stop me, "Jon your dad said..."

"I know what the coach said. And what the coach said will kill us!"

With that, I kept walking till I got to the cooler. And I took a cup. And I took a drink. And another. And another. One by one, each player dropped their ball and walked their dry throats over to the cooler. I held out a cup and someone took it and drank. And then the next guy and then the next until they all drank. And kept drinking. Ben took a cup of water and threw it over his head to cool down the overheating.

All this time Coach was watching us through the

office window. And we knew it.

NOT DAD...COACH

His office door opened and he came walking across the floor. There was anger in his steps.

"I see you took a water break. So I would assume that you made thirty free throws in a row. Is that correct?" He was staring at me. The silence seemed eternal.

Finally someone answered, "No sir we did not."

"Well then there must have been some misunderstanding about my instructions. Because I am sure that I said no water till you do. Was I not clear?"

"You were sir."

With that, dad grabbed the cooler and threw it to the ground, breaking the lid. Water spilled all over the floor while we looked on in shock. "Ok then. Since you want to defy me, shuttle runs. Everybody on the line. I'm gonna run you till you drop!"

Every face in the gym was dejected. We had just finished practice, every player tired. I could not make the whole team pay for something I had done. "Dad it was not them it was me. I told them to drink the water."

He glared at me with a frigid stare, and, for what seemed like an eternity, said nothing. It wasn't disappointment I saw in his eyes. Disappointment still speaks of emotion and he was past that. He stared at me as if I were no longer his son.

"Jon. On the line."

Thirty

"But dad?"

"On the line boy!"

With my teammates watching from the side, I walked over to the line, and he ran me. Full court. Baseline to free throw. Baseline to half court. Opposite free throw. Opposite baseline.

"Again." Full court. Baseline to free throw. Baseline to half court. Opposite free throw. Opposite baseline.

"Again."

The first three were bearable. The fourth, fifth and sixth hurt. The seventh…on the seventh, I heard Ben's stuttering voice. I think its Ben. My head is spinning. I collapse to the floor.

"S-S-Stop! Stop o-or I quit!" That was not his nature. Ben was a soft-spoken, skinny giant, his 6'6" frame not matching his gentle personality. "If you don't stop right now, I'll…I'll, I will never p-p-play for you again. He is my teammate. He is our leader. And he is your s-son!"

Ben walked over to where I was and tried to help me up off the ground. Then, one after the next, my teammates stepped forward and stood beside me.

"Me too."

"Me too."

He stared at them, and then at me. "Don't ever call me dad at a practice again. When you are on this court you call me coach!" He dropped his whistle and stalked out of the gym.

I recovered. We always do. But I never called him dad in that gym again.

I Am Jon

1 SAMUEL 16
14 *At that very moment the Spirit of God left Saul and in its place a black mood sent by God settled on him. He was terrified.*
15-16 *Saul's advisors said, "This awful tormenting depression from God is making your life miserable. O Master, let us help. Let us look for someone who can play the harp. When the black mood from God moves in, he'll play his music and you'll feel better."*

1 SAMUEL 16
18 *One of the young men spoke up, "I know someone. The son of Jesse of Bethlehem, an excellent musician. He's also courageous, of age, well-spoken, and good-looking. And God is with him."*
19 *So Saul sent messengers to Jesse requesting, "Send your son David to me, the one who tends the sheep."*

Chapter 5

HELP NEEDED

Dad and I never mentioned that day. It was as if it never happened, at least in his mind. But for me, it was a bad memory tattooed on my brain. I would lay in my bed at night unable to sleep, his words on repeat in my mind. Words hurt. And his words hurt me deep. I loved him still, though. And I knew for sure, that he loved me.

I could tell he felt bad and wanted to say sorry. But sometimes saying I'm sorry is hard. And some people are really not good at it. So dad did his best. But what came out was some strange beast—half apology, half explanation, and a whole lot of excuse. I was sitting at the small table in the corner of the kitchen, and he walked in. He didn't open a cupboard or go to the fridge. He just stood there. Right behind me. Seemed as if he had something he wanted to say. But based on our last conversation, I wasn't too sure I wanted to hear it. So I buried my nose in my cereal as deep as it could go, hoping the bowl would give me cover.

He started into a conversation as though he was

continuing a dialogue that we actually never had. "See Jon, about yesterday, I think I'm really stressed, and I know why. I've just got too much to do. Too much to think about. I've got so many little things that I have to do that I can't sit and concentrate on what I need to do. Figure out how to beat Coastal."

"I sit in my office, and I draw a hundred plays, and then I trash every single one of them. I come home at night and skip dinner to plan practice. I fall asleep watching film, studying their players and their plays. Did you know that I sent Tony to their gym to secretly record some of their practices?"

"Dad!" He ignored my shock.

"Jon, every night I wake up in cold sweats after dreaming the same dream. I am old, and I'm walking through a town. I think its Dyer. I walk past the Corner Store. It's empty. Past the park. No one there. No cars at the gas station. No one anywhere. Everyone is in our gym. There is a crowd. I walk into the gym and start talking to people, but they can't hear me. They can't see me either. The people start walking through me like I'm not even there. Like I don't matter. And then I wake up. Jon if we don't beat Coastal, I'm afraid I won't matter. I will be remembered as the coach that couldn't get it done. I've got to find a way to beat Coastal. We have got to beat those Giants."

And there it was. Straight from his mouth. He was possessed by the thought of beating Coastal. It's one thing to have a drive to win. But it's another when that

Help Needed

drive has you, when ambition has you, because you will hate what you become. Without a doubt, he was possessed by that drive. And the longer it possessed him, the worse things got for us. There was a dark, low-hanging fog taking over him, and the gym, and the team. Our home. We all knew that something had to change. Something had to break it.

"Dad, I just think you are doing too much." Here I go, offering my opinion again. As if I didn't know how this would turn out. But I love him and just can't help myself. "You are doing everything— You prepare for practices. You teach classes. You clean the gym. You pump the balls. You wash the uniforms. You prep the locker. You deposit the booster money."

"There's really not a lot for me to do with that last job now, is there? When is the last time the boosters gave me money?" We laughed. It felt good to laugh with my dad.

"Dad, you are doing too much. And we all feel it. I feel it. You are shouting at the players, screaming at refs. You got into it last week with Jude's mom."

"She was asking for it. She is always interrupting practice, always asking me questions to try to show me up."

"Dad it was after practice in the parking lot. And she was asking you if she could bring cake to the next practice to celebrate Jude's birthday! You are just out of control sometimes... a lot of times."

He knew that what I was saying was true. He felt the darkness too. He knew that the fun was gone. So this time, he didn't turn away. There was no sarcastic eye roll. He was looking me in the face as if he wanted my answer. I think I had his ear.

"You need someone to take some of that stuff off your hands, to relieve some of the pressure so that you can go back to being the coach we all love... the coach we all want to play for...the coach I respect and love. My dad. You need help."

DEE

The days that followed mushed into the mundane. Nothing much changed. Dad and the team seemed to settle on an unspoken agreement. He would barely coach, and we would barely play. Both of us acted as if we were on punishment, forced to be there, no one happy. Dad had lost his passion, and we had lost our drive. Practices were now degraded to playlists from some YouTube channel. Fact. One day coach walked into the gym with a laptop, pressed play, said "do this and when you are done go home." I don't think any of us bothered to finish the workout. We walked out of the gym, leaving the video playing on the floor.

But there was more. It wasn't now just his lack of focus or his poorly organized practices, or even his temper tantrums. What was had developed into something else. His mood—it became dark, distant,

Help Needed

depressed, unfamiliar. Dad stopped talking to friends. Stopped taking phone calls. He came home and just sat in his chair in the corner, sometimes never turning on a light. I was worried.

Then one day, Ben, the tall guy who stuttered, was late. "Hey Jon, where's Ben?"

"Not sure."

"Izzie have you heard anything from Ben?"

"No coach."

"Has anybody on this team heard from Ben?"

None of us had heard from him, and that was strange because Ben was never late. Can't tell you what anybody else was thinking, but I got to thinking that he probably just quit. Wasn't like the rest of us had not thought about it.

Ten minutes later, in walked Ben. No running. No hustle. Just a slow, hunched stroll. And there was someone walking behind him. Coach stomped in his direction. The painful punishment for his transgression was already locked and loaded.

"Ben this better be good. If not…. Who is that? Is he with you?"

"Yes s-s-sir he's m-my little brother. And it ain't even my fault!"

Ben's stutter was always worse under pressure, and he knew team rules. Being late was a big no-no, the magnitude of which was only surpassed by bringing outsiders to practice. Coach didn't like people coming to practice because he said outsiders were a distraction. Said he couldn't share our attention with anybody else and get stuff done. But privately, he admitted that he was really concerned about Coastal spies. I now knew that was most likely because he had spies of his own in their gym.

"Coach, my momma sent him to practice. He wasn't doing nothing at home anyway, just playing on that computer. And she wasn't having it. So she made me bring him. I told her that you don't like that, but she said, 'You tell the coach I said put him to work. He's a strong boy. Find him something to do. Then tell him that I said either he goes with you to practice or you ain't going at all. It's a package deal.' And coach you know how my momma be. I ain't got no choice." Ben was right. We all knew his mom. Nice lady. But she was no joke!

His brother was a good kid. Freshman. Everybody loved him. We all knew about him even before he came to our school because he was always hanging around his big brother. When we were younger, we grew up playing ball in Twelve Points Park. And whenever Ben showed up, he was always there, wanting to play, wishing he could play. But he was small. Way too small. We had wondered how he and Ben could come from the same family. And he wasn't just short. He was short and scrawny. A lightweight. So we shoved him to the side, told him to go shoot on his own and work on his game. Then maybe, we would let him play. He did go practice, but we would never let him into the game.

It had been a few years since. And nature had

Help Needed

been kind to the kid, though not generous. He was no longer small or scrawny. And though his brother still towered over him, it was in a less than laughable sort of way. Plus, based on where he started, he was blessed to be even a notch north of average.

"Son what's your name?"

"People call me Dee, sir."

"Dee, am I to understand that you were misbehaving?"

"No sir." Ben jumped in. "He was not misbehaving. Just on that computer all the time. And when he ain't on that computer, he just talks too much, asks too many questions. Way too many questions. He can't help himself. Asking questions and telling jokes. That's all this boy do. Gets on my momma's last nerve. So she said he had to find something productive to do with himself, something good to do with all his energy. 'Cause no son of mine gonna spend all day on that computer!' That's what she said, Coach."

"Dee is that right?"

"Yes sir."

"Call me coach. Son, why are you torturing your mom with all your talking? You're killing her peace. What's wrong with you...can't you be quiet?"

"Well sir, coach, with all due respect, I like asking questions, cause if you don't ask questions, you will only know what you know, and you never know what you don't. And jokes? I like telling jokes...just cause."

"Well Dee, I don't normally let people sit in on our practices, but we need your brother, and I'm not about to fight your mom. So you can go over there and sit on those bleachers and be quiet. No jokes. And no questions. Can you do that?"

"Yes sir I can… but before I go over there, can I tell you a joke?"

"And here you go with the questions and the jokes. I knew this was a bad idea."

But Dee just forged ahead: "What's the difference between bird flu and swine flu?"

"Boy I don't know."

"One requires a tweetment and the other requires an oinkment!"

There was silence. Dad just stared at him with squinted eyes for what seemed like forever, and none of us dared laugh. Then, on the outer regions of his mouth, I saw a slight curl. From his belly I heard a rumble. And then, finally, a soft but very distinct chuckle. We all heard it. And when we did, every player exploded in raucous laughter. Gathering his defenses, once more, dad motioned, "Get over there to those bleachers. No more questions and no more jokes. Y'all get on the line. Everybody is running suicides cause Ben was late."

Dad walked away shaking his head, stepped into his office, and slammed the door. But we saw him through the office window—back arched, one hand on his desk, the other on his stomach.

Help Needed

The glass and the walls were unable to contain his laughter. "Tweetment and Oinkment!"

We lined up and ran our suicides. But those were the happiest suicides we would ever run.

I Am Jon

1 SAMUEL 16

20-21 *Jesse sent his son to Saul. David came to Saul and stood before him. Saul liked him immediately and made him his right-hand man.*

23 *After that, whenever the bad depression from God tormented Saul, David got out his harp and played. That would calm Saul down, and he would feel better as the moodiness lifted.*

Chapter 6

ONE OF US

I guess Ben's mom liked her 2 1/2 hours of peace because after that day, Dee was always at our practices. Not sure if he was coming because he liked it or because he was forced, but that didn't much matter to me. Having him around was a good thing. A really good thing. There was something about him. It was more than the talking, more than the jokes or the awkward funny faces. There was something different about his spirit, something that strolled in with him the way he had strolled in with Ben. And whatever that thing was, it left with him when he left.

To be honest, the only person that struggled with Dee's presence was Ben, and I got it. I understood why. It would have been tough for me to never get a break from my little brother. A little brother that had a way of taking over a room, filling it to the point of leaving me forgettable. But we loved Ben, and he knew it, so I guess he tolerated Dee's presence.

Even coach liked having Dee at practice, though he would never say it.

"You again?"

I Am Jon

"Yes sir. Mr. Coach, sir. You ain't getting rid of me! My momma gonna make sure of that. She gotta have her two hours of peace. And she ain't gonna get no peace with me round asking questions now is she? And I know you wouldn't want to take my momma's peace now would ya?"

"Boy get in them bleachers, and I don't want to hear a peep from you during my practice. Ya hear?"

Dee stood at attention and gave coach his best salute, "Yes sir!"

And Dee pretty much stuck to his word. We heard very little from his perch in the bleachers during the practice. A few claps and "ohs" here and there for a great play or good shot, but not much more. But as soon as the final whistle blew, and the practice was over, the gym was his. We called it the Dee Show. He freed himself from bleacher exile and followed us into the locker room, stood on a bench and hurled jokes till our bellies hurt.

"What did the Buffalo say to his son when he left for college?"

"What?"

"Bi-son!"

"What does a nosey pepper do?"

"We don't know? What?"

"Get jalapeño business!"

"Dee where do you get all these jokes?"

"Duh! The internet!"

We all roared.

And that became our thing. We practiced, and then

we laughed. The harder the practice, the more we needed to laugh. The more we laughed, the harder we wanted to practice. It was weird, but it worked. The darkness was lifting, and everybody noticed, including coach. So the next day, right at the beginning of practice, he called up to the bird in the bleachers.

"Dee get down here!"

"Coach what did I do? I ain't laugh. I ain't cough. It was my breathing, right? Do I breathe too loud? I knew I should have never taken that last breath!"

"Boy can you be quiet even for a moment?"

The coach and Dee were now standing in the middle of a circle that formed around them. I didn't know what dad was going to do. Why did he call Dee to the floor? My gut didn't trust it. Neither did the guts of anybody else in the gym whose name wasn't Coach. And we had reason. We had seen him murder fun before. But this was different because what Dee brought was not just fun. Dee brought life! We needed him. My mind was racing; my heart was cold. Was he about to kick him out of the gym? Tell him never to come back? Would we have to defend Dee the way the team defended me? If so, we are ready to riot because...

"Boys, I know that things been a little rough round here lately." Nervous laugh. "We kinda been off our game a bit. Well not, not really, we...me. I've been off my game. Not been the kind of coach you boys deserve, and I don't have any excuses. Now I've been coaching most of you for a while, and you know that

I preach that one of the four pillars of success in anything is accountability. And accountability cuts both ways. I ask you to be on time, to know your assignments, to practice your craft. And you expect me to lead this team. Well, I have not been much of a leader lately. So I am asking you for your forgiveness and asking each of you to give me another chance."

Silence. Stunned. "I been thinking about it for a while and I talked to a guy that I think is pretty wise." Dad is staring right at me. "He said I needed some help." Dad turned to Dee. "Dee do you know how to pump balls?"

"Yes Sir."

"Can you sweep a floor?"

"Yes Sir."

"If I showed you how, could you wash the uniforms and lay them out before games? Could you make sure that the team bench is out, and the water cooler is full?"

"Yes Sir."

"And if I was running late, could I give you the warmup drills and ask you to warm up the team?",

With every question Dee's chest got higher. His smile lit the gym. "Yes Sir."

"And Dee, when I get a little too serious and cranky, and practice feels yucky could you tell us one of your jokes?"

"For sure coach!"

"Good. Now team, I know you have taken a liking to Dee, and I don't want to make this decision all by

One Of Us

myself. But would you mind if I asked Dee to be our team manager? Dee, we want you to be one of us."

With that, dad dug into a bag he was holding and pulled out a jacket in Providence purple, a letterman one. On the chest, it said "Team Manager." And on the back, in big, bold letters "DEE". "If you gonna be one of us, you've got to look like one of us."

Dee was silent. Watering eyes fixed on that jacket. "Now, I spent a lot of money on this jacket, son, so you can't say no. What do you say?"

He wiped a tear and said in the softest voice I had ever heard issued from his mouth, "Yes sir. Yes sir, coach. It would be an honor!" The response from the team was deafening. We shouted. We screamed. We high-fived.

"Seems as though they want you around, son. They need you. I need you! Welcome to the team! Ok. It's time to get to practice, but before we get started, I got a joke of my own. What did the cobbler say to the cat that came into his shop?"

"What coach?"

"Shoe!"

We roared even though I am pretty sure no one knew what a cobbler was. Or why a cat would bother to go into his store. But none of that mattered. Dad was telling corny jokes again, and that was reason enough to laugh.

That evening after practice, Dee did what Dee had always done. He got up on a bench in the locker room and told us his jokes. Only this time, dad was in the back of the room, clapping and laughing with us.

The next day went as the day before. And the day before that. And the day before that. School had become monotonous, a repeating of routines so predictable that you could walk through the day with your eyes closed. The gathering in the halls to talk about the last night's activities: "Did you watch...?"

"Did you hear...?"

"I went here."

"I went there."

"I did all of my homework."

"I did none of my homework."

Its eight o'clock. Bell rings. School begins. Mrs. Kent excitedly chats about the twists and turns of William Shakespeare too early in the morning, again. The rest of us still wonder who's taking who's pound of flesh. Mr. Schuler gives a surprise quiz in second period World History, again. And the only person surprised is him. Everyone knows he gives quizzes when he needs more time to figure out what he is gonna teach that day—mostly on Thursdays after late Wednesday night bowling. Frankie Foster misses that surprise quiz, again, but that's no surprise because Frankie is always late. We stand in the lunch line reaching for cardboard pizza and cold fries, again. The only saving grace for my day was sitting with Michal at the corner table by the windows. Somehow, we were able to find enough humor to survive the monotony.

"When's the last time they changed the menu," I complained.

"Man, nothing in this place changes."

"You would think that somebody would have tasted the pizza by now. Everybody throws it in the garbage, and it's not because we aren't hungry."

Lunch is over too soon. Afternoon classes drag on for too long. Mr. Garcia is frustrated because we still can't roll Spanish r's. Ms. Smith teaches Trigonometry with the enthusiasm of a pet rock. The only saving grace—Michal and I have the same classes.

"Michal! Why is PE at the end of the day? Who has energy for all that movement after being at school all day?"

"I know. I know. And someone needs to tell the P.E. teacher that this is not the military."

"That woman is a beast," I said.

"One more push-up and I promise you, my arms would have exploded."

And so the day goes. Bell rings. School is over. Thank God! A slow wading through the halls, making sure you talk to all your people and catch the eye of your interest. For me and my teammates that wading eventually leads us back to the dark hallway that leads to the dusty gym for practice, again. Always seemed like a punishment.

But that day something would change. Before we even reached the gym, we heard strange sounds seeping under the gaps in the door. None of us could

I Am Jon

tell exactly what it was, but it sounded like music. The guys were genuinely afraid, and they turned to me for explanation.

"Jon do you know about this? What's your dad up to now? He's been acting really strange lately."

"Guys, I promise you, I am as lost as you are. If I knew, I promise I would have told you."

There was real fear in Dan's eyes, "Well what do you think it is? I ain't going in there till somebody tells me what's going on. This could be some sick drill. And I just don't have the energy to go through that again today."

"Guys, calm down. It's just music. If we keep standing out here talking, we are going to be late. And if we are late, practice is gonna be painful for sure, so let's just go in."

Just then, we heard quick and heavy footsteps approaching behind us. I looked over my shoulder. It was dad.

Eyebrows raised. Jaws dropped. If he is out here with us, who is that in the gym? "What's going on here. Why are all you guys just standing out here in the hall? And what is that noise coming from the gym? If this is some type of practical joke, you guys are gonna wish you were never born." He pushed past us and blasted through the gym door. Dad stopped just inside of the door and was silent. Slowly, we shuffled in behind him.

Light. There was so much light. You could feel the light on your face.

One Of Us

"Hope you guys like what I did to the place. Just needed a little sprucing up, that's all." Dee. He was walking toward us from the locker rooms in the corner, wearing the jacket dad gave him, smiling like he knew he'd done something good. "Wanted to do more, but y'all will have to forgive me. I'm still a rookie manager."

Silence. No one said anything. There was just silence. Except for the music. We were all just taking it in. The floor was swept and shiny. Light bulbs that had been blown were replaced. But the light in the room was not from the bulbs. There were windows at the very top of the gym that had been covered with bleached curtains for as long as I could remember. I think their original purpose was to stop the glare of the light on the floor or something. They had been there so long, and they were so high, almost touching the ceiling, that no one ever thought about taking them down.

"The windows. I didn't even remember they were there," Dad said staring at the windows in an arrested gaze.

"Well sir, people get used to living in the dark."

"But how did you get up there?"

"Well, I pulled out the bleachers and set an 18-foot ladder on the top row. But I think we had better keep that between us. Cause if my mother knew, she would kill me, and then she would kill you."

The score board was on. The timer was out. Dee had even laid out our practice jerseys at our locker

I Am Jon

spaces. And the music...

"Did you skip classes to do this young man? Cause if you did, you..."

"No sir, coach sir. I never skip classes. My last two periods were open today, so I asked my teacher if I could come take care of my duties. She let me go. She likes my jokes."

"Boy, don't you lie to me. You did not do all of this in two class periods."

"Ok coach. You got me. You right. I came in last night since there was no practice. Gave myself a head start. The janitor let me in. He happens to like my jokes too. So what do you think?"

"What's that noise I'm hearing?"

"Well coach, I ain't been on the job long..."

"Exactly 2 days!"

"Yeah coach It's only been two days. But it's been my observation that things around here are a little drab. No energy. And it is impossible to shape these boys into the elite athletes they are supposed to be in these conditions. If we want to get the best outta this team, we are gonna have to provide them with the right working environment. Now you do know that music has the ability to raise workout intensity, thus resulting in better workouts and improved performance, right?"

"And where did you get that information?"

"Google, of course. So I made an executive decision as the new manager of this franchise," pointing to the title 'manager' embroidered on his chest, "and

One Of Us

I decided that since pre and post practice time is mine, I'm gonna play music. I put together a playlist on my phone. Uh coach, a playlist is a..."

"I know what a playlist is young man."

"So proud of you coach. Yeah. So this is a playlist of my favorite Jesus music. Gets me going every time. Hit ya with the hype stuff at the top to get the boys all fired up, and the mellow stuff on the end is for the cool down. I hope you don't mind."

"Dee, I didn't know you were Christian."

"You never asked coach. There are a lot of things about me you don't know." Dee wheeled around, searching the group of boys standing behind coach looking giddy.

"Dan, you look thirsty. You should go get you some water."

"Actually I'm not. I brought my own water."

"Dan, you should go get water...from the water fountain, Dan."

Dee was wearing the largest smile I had ever seen on a face. Must have been infectious because soon, Dan was wearing that smile too.

"No way!"

"Yes way, Dan. Go get some water from the water fountain."

Dan walked over to the fountain slowly pressed the button and... water. Ice cold water spurting from that broken water fountain. Dan is dancing.

"And it's clean too. This is unbelievable!"

"Dee you know how to fix water fountains?"

"Of course not, coach. I just know how to call a plumber. His bill is on your desk." We all fell on the floor laughing.

"Alright. Alright. Boys, let's clap it up for our manager here. He did pretty good for a rookie. But Dee you better never, ever, never think about spending money without talking to me first. Now enough with the concert and comedy. Let's get to work."

Chapter 7

SHARE THE MIC

I know I've said it before, but I need to say it again. Everything changed the day Dee walked into our gym. Everything. He was literally our inspiration, seemingly an answer to all that had been wrong for so long. I guess sometimes breaking the monotony is not as hard as you think. Just one unexpected, inspired change.

But what kept gnawing at me was why. What was it that he was doing? How was it that his presence made such an amazing difference in coach and in us? I gotta admit that a part of my bother was the fact that there was another voice in the gym, whose words had weight. I was used to being that voice. In the absence of dad, I was the one that the team turned to for everything. And I realized that I rather liked being depended on, called on, in charge. But now the stage was not mine alone, and sometimes I found myself fighting to get that microphone back. But the more I fought, the more it slipped from my hand.

"What time is our game tomorrow? Can't find my schedule."

I Am Jon

"No one is surprised, Izzie. You would lose your head if it wasn't connected to your neck."

"Ha ha. Funny. Now does anyone actually have an answer to my question."

I said, "The game is at 5:00 Izzie, like every other home game we've played this season."

"Actually the game is at 5:30 Jon. Middleton asked us to delay the game by thirty minutes. Something about roadwork on the interstate."

Did Dee just correct me? "When did this change?"

"Yesterday. Coach and I discussed it."

"When was I gonna find out?"

"I don't know. I guess when he announced it to the team. But Izzie, coach wants the team here at regular team check in time."

"That's 4 o'clock!" I inserted. I'm starting to get annoyed.

"Well actually, Jon, that was the old check-in time. Remember last week we decided that the team needed an hour and a half to dress and warm up instead of an hour. So check-in time is 3:30."

"Why am I just hearing about this?"

"I'm not sure. I sent it out in the team's email blast... And by the way, none of you guys responded to the joke? 'Jesus said Lazarus come forth and he got a new life. The guy who came fifth just got a toaster.' Hilarious huh?"

"I didn't say nothing cause I didn't get it. Who is Lazarus?"

"Izzie you should try going to church at least once

in your life."

"I've been to church, thank you very much."

The whole team was laughing. I was not.

"Wait we have an email blast now?"

"Yeah Jon. I'm just trying to make sure that everybody is getting the same information."

To be honest I was steaming on the inside. How is this little ball boy telling me about what's happening with my team. Couldn't keep it in. "Why are you being included in all this stuff? You just need to do your job. You are not really the manager Dee. You are just a ball boy. So pump the balls and fill water jugs and stop trying to act like you're more important than you are!"

Those words were poison. The moment they left my mouth, I regretted it. I had shown my hand. I was jealous. But more than that, I had embarrassed Dee in front of the team, and that was not cool. "I'm sorry."

"It's cool Jon. Ben does me way worse." He smiled one of those hurt smiles. "I'll make sure to talk to you first before I send anything to the team. You deserve that. You are our leader. Was never my intent to disrespect you."

He picked up the towels on the floor and walked back to the locker room. I felt horrible. But the grace that he gave me in that moment only made me feel worse. When you know that you deserve to be screamed at, and you expect a fight, yet what you receive instead is mercy, it can humble the wildest ego. And that is what I felt. Humbled. But it only made me even more curious. How could this kid be so mature? He was just a jokester that strayed into the gym one day, right? I was really puzzled.

So I waited to talk to him after practice, after everyone else left. I knew he would be there a little longer, setting up the bleachers for the game.

"Thought you could use a hand."

"Sure Jon. I could always use another pair."

I walked over and leaned on the bleacher he was pushing and gave it my shoulder.

"I am really sorry about what I said today. It was completely out of line. You did not deserve that."

"Don't worry about it, Jon. I forgave you as soon as you said it."

I stopped pushing. Confused look. "Why would you do that?"

"What?"

"Forgive me before I even apologized?"

"Cause I know what it is like to need forgiveness. So I forgive, knowing that at some point, I'm gonna need forgiveness again. Plus, when you hold on to grudges, they can burn holes in your hand."

"What website did you get that from?"

"I got it from me."

"You are strange."

"Thank you."

That night, Michal came over to bring me the trigonometry book I had left at school. We sat on the driveway for a while as I recounted what had

Share The Mic

happened in the gym that day.
 "You must have felt like trash."
 "Yeah. That's about right."
 "He sounds like a pretty special kid."
 "He is. He really is."

Chapter 8

LET YOUR LION ROAR

So things got better in practice. A lot better. Spirits were higher. Dad was more relaxed. The team was more engaged. Dad decided to lower the admission to our home games to $2 for the community and free for students, which put a few more people in the seats. That was all good.

But nothing improved on the court. At best, we were a middle of the road team. Good enough to beat bad teams. Bad enough to lose to good teams. Lucky enough to win a few more than we would lose. Worse, the team was also paper thin. We had enough decent players to wear jerseys, but with all the transfers, we could not afford another injury. And another injury is exactly what we got.

Coach had been encouraging Ben to get more aggressive. "Ben, you are just too nice."

"Sorry Coach."

"If I had your height, I would've been clearing bodies out of the paint. Nobody would even think about coming in here for a layup. But the way you play, you are like the Jolly Green Giant, smiling and stuff, apologizing when you foul people. Forget that man!"

"Sorry Coach."

Ben's head hung low; eyes stuck on his laces. He looked lost. He wasn't quite comfortable with what coach was asking him to do. He had always been that nice guy, the kid that screamed, "Sorry!" every time he crashed into someone at bumper cars or rubbed shoulders in a crowd. He didn't have a mean bone in his body. So to him, coach was asking him to be someone he wasn't.

"Coach let me try." Dee walked over to his brother. "Ben, you remember Momma telling us the story about Jesus being the Lamb of God, right?"

"Uh huh."

"Well, in another part of the Bible, it describes Him as the Lion of Judah."

"Uh huh."

"He is both a Lion and a Lamb, Ben."

"Ok."

"Ben, when you off this court, you can be a lamb, if you want. Be a nice guy. Say sorry and all that…" All of a sudden it felt like we were sitting in church, cause Dee put on a preacher's voice, and we were all shouting, "Yes!", "Uh-huh!"

"But when you hit this court…"

"Yes!"

"And the ref throws that ball in the air…"

"Yes!"

"You got to have a mean streak in you, bro." Someone shouted "Hallelujah!"

"Lemme hear your lion roar."

"Amen!"

"Roar bro."

"You preaching Dee."

Dee was now face-to-chest with his brother, and he pounded that chest with every word: "You be nice off the court if you want, bro, but out here on this court, you got to make them fear you! You got to let your lion roar! Roar Ben, roar!"

With that, the whole team roared with approval. Dee backed away from Ben, mean faced, never losing eye contact with him and said, "Is that what you were trying to say coach?"

My dad had the most confused look on his face.

"Not... in... so many words, Dee, but yes, I guess."

None of us were really sure if he got the message. We saw no real sign of change until one evening a few practices later. We had practiced pretty hard. Coach had been riding Ben for his lack of energy on the court again. Nothing new. I shot the ball. It bounced off for a rebound. Simon thought he had it. Casually jumped to grab it. He never saw Ben coming till he heard a primal scream, "AHHHHHHHH. My ball!"

Ben grabbed that rebound, elbows swinging, legs kicking, mean face. And in the process, ran right through Simon. Simon crashed to the floor and let out a scream of his own. Only, his was of sheer pain.

"Ben. What'd you do that for?" coach yelled, running toward SImon's crumpled body.

"I-I-I was letting my lion roar, coach, just like you told me."

Simon slowly got up off the floor, threw a dirty look Ben's way, and hobbled to the bench. He was clearly in a lot of pain. Unable to continue. This was our last practice before our next game, and that opponent was a tough one. Coach was just getting into the set plays and details of the game plan. We had to finish, but we needed ten players to do it. He stood there for a while, hand on hips, staring at the floor. We waited.

"Dee jump in."

"Me coach?"

"Yes you. You been here long enough. You know the plays. You can just fill the space. You don't really have to shoot. Just stand there."

"Coach, I'm the manager."

"The manager's job is to do what I tell them to do. And today, I'm telling the manager to get on the court. So take off your jacket, find a practice jersey and get out there. You are playing at the 2."

"2?"

"Just go stand next to Jon Dee." The boys were hooting and hollering.

Even Simon wobbled to his feet, waving a towel in the air. "Let's go Dee! Let's go!"

Slowly, he peeled off his manager's jacket, glanced over at Ben, and got on the court looking nervous. I walked over to where he was standing and said, "Don't worry Dee. It's just practice. You can't mess

I Am Jon

up. Just follow my lead, and you'll do ok." He gave me a nod.

We ran through the drill the first time. I called a screen play where Dee barely had to move and never touched the ball. We ran it a second, third time. Much the same. Every time we got through a play, guys high-fived Dee as though he had hit a game-winning shot. We started to run a 30-second shot clock drill where we practiced running the play and getting up a good shot before the shot clock expired. Coach hated when this drill was not run right. We often paid for it with push-ups. So things on the court got a little more focused, more intense. The first few times through, we did fine. Dee's task was simple: run to the corner and stand outside of the three-point line. The ball generally never went there. But on the last play, the ball somehow ended up in Dee's hands with 5 seconds left on the clock, and there was no time for him to pass to anyone else. "Shoot Dee! You got to put up a shot!"

The look on his face said that he wasn't expecting it. Wasn't even facing the rim. Didn't think he would even have to touch the ball, far less shoot. But he turned and got the shot off. Kinda. It was ugly. Laughable. Like a flying chicken with two broken feet and one broken wing. No conceivable shooting form. No ball rotation. Dee's shot hit the rim so hard it almost left a dent.

"Stop. Now you tell me how that ball ended up in Dee's hands with 5 seconds to go? How? He can't make that shot, so why pass him the ball? That play was supposed to go to the other side. You can't still be making these kind of mistakes. Everybody down and give me 20 push-ups!" Moans. Players painfully made their way to the floor and got into a push-up position.

Dee just stood there. "You too Dee. You play with the team, you pay with the team!"

Dee didn't move. "I can."

"What was that?"

"I can hit that shot."

Coach walked over toward Dee. "Listen son. Just because you are wearing a jersey now doesn't mean you are a player. As soon as this practice is over that jersey comes off and that manager jacket goes back on."

"I might not be a player to you, coach. But I know I can hit that shot."

"You are arrogant!"

"No sir. I am confident. My momma told me a long time ago, I can do all things through Christ who gives me strength."

"Here you go with that church stuff again. You need to leave that stuff in the pews, son. This is a basketball court."

"Coach God is the God of the pew and the court. All things mean all things."

Coach stared at him for a second. "Ok, Dee. You hit that shot, and no one does push-ups. You miss and everyone does double." Coach put him back in the corner and gave him the ball. "It's all on you Dee."

The team was no longer in push-up position. Most were on their knees, probably praying for a miracle. Dee stood there a second and took a deep breath. Set his feet. Ugly form. Released the ball. Ball hit the rim. Ball rolled around rim. Through the net.

Every player jumped to their feet and mobbed Dee. He looked at us, looked at coach and shouted, "Providence, repeat after me. I can."

"I can."
"Do all things."
"Do all things."
"Everything."
"Everything."
"Anything."
"Anything."
"Through Christ."
"Through Christ."
"Through Christ."
"Through Christ."
"He strengthens me."
"He strengthens me."[1]
"Now, let your lion roar."
"AHHHHHHHHHH!!"

---

1 Philippians 4:13

Chapter 9

WHAT JUST HAPPENED

That moment. I don't think that I can really describe it. It was, powerful. Raw. In the moment, we were all hyped, jumping around, going crazy. But as the energy faded, questions remained. What really happened? This kid who walked in off the street and into our gym had just made a shot under extreme pressure, and he did not even flinch. Who was he? How did he hit that shot? Something in his eyes told me that he believed that he could make that shot over and over again. How was he so confident? All these questions. All this confusion. Intrigue. I wanted to know him and understand him.

All night, questions screamed. My mind was never silent, and it wouldn't be until I got answers. So the next day, I waited for him at his locker. Must have looked like a stalker. I didn't even say hi. "How did you do that?"

"What?"

"Yesterday!"

"Oh that. That was pretty cool, huh? Well, I set my feet and..." He was now showing me his shooting form.

"That is not what I mean, and you know it! Weren't you scared?"

"Scared of what?"

"Failing. Scared of looking bad. Scared to be wrong."

"No."

"But how?"

He opened his locker and grabbed a book. "I don't believe in failing. At least not the way most people do."

"What do you mean?"

"First of all, if I set out to do something, and it doesn't work, just means there is something for me to learn. Second, somebody told me the only people who fail are the people who don't try. Plus I figured I could use some push-ups. Have you seen my muscles?"

"See that's what I'm talking about. Where do you get that stuff from? Ninth graders don't talk like that. And the chant. Where did that come from?"

"Oh that. That was scripture. From the Bible. God's book? Moses? Baby Jesus?"

"I know what the Bible is, Dee. I meant where did you learn it?"

"Oh, Sam taught me."

"Sam?"

"Sam is the youth pastor at the church down the street. You know, the one across from the park. He is kinda like a mentor ya know?"

Of course I knew that church. Everybody did. No

What Just Happened

one knew what type of church it was — Baptist or Adventist or whatever other kind of "ist" they have in church world. We all just called it The Church at the Park. I think every kid in town had taken their turn to jump that church's fence into the old graveyard where some stray fly ball was rested between two tombstones. There were stories about kids who climbed over and never came back. Now that I was older, I knew they were a joke, but when I was younger, those stories scared the good sense out of me.

"He says memorizing scripture makes you strong on the inside, so he gives me something to remember every week. That one is the one I like the most. Philippians 4:13, I think. So I am always repeating it. Been saying it to myself before all my tests, especially algebra. Lord have mercy! That thing is of the devil. But in the moment, it was what was in me, so I guess it just popped out."

He didn't flinch when he talked about church, and I wasn't used to that. At least, not from anybody else. Everybody at Providence knew where I stood, but for the most part, I stood alone. I knew for a fact that there were other Christians at the school, but none of them wanted anyone else to know. Ask them what they did on weekends, and they talked about everything, except church, almost as though they were ashamed.

But Dee didn't try to hide it. Wasn't embarrassed. Didn't stutter. In fact, he said what he said with a boldness that made being a Christian sound cool. And because he was so bold with his faith, he made everyone around him want to be a believer too. If what I saw in him was a result of this guy Sam, I wanted to meet him.

"Sam sounds like a cool guy."

"He's the best. He meets me at the park, and we just kinda hang and talk. We talk about everything. School. Life. God. He really believes in me. He always says he thinks that I was born to do something big, that God has plans for me. Never had no one talk to me like that before. No one ever really expected me to do anything important. But he's been pouring this stuff into my head and holding me accountable for becoming the dude he sees. To be honest, wasn't that sure at first. Kept thinking 'what's this guy's angle?' But he's been consistent, always there. And he's been telling me this stuff for so long now, I am actually starting to believe it."

"What did he say you were born to do?"

"Didn't say. Don't think he really knows. But he said that I don't need to know. When it's time, God will show me. Till then, I just gotta live every day as though today will be the day, and make God proud while doing it. That includes folding towels and pumping balls and taking shots and doing algebra. That reminds me, gotta go. Never sure if Ms. Smith is gonna give a pop quiz, so I can't be late. See ya at practice!"

Dee bounced away. Then he turned around and

shouted back, "You should meet Sam. He's a really cool dude. Think you would like him."

"Sure. Yeah. Whenever. Hey but the shot. How did you hit the shot?"

Bell rung, and the hallway was flooded with bodies. Not sure if Dee heard me. He was swallowed up so quickly by the ocean of students heading to their next class, that he left that last question unanswered. But that was the first question I had asked right? And still it was the one that remained. Was he trying to avoid the answer?

I know it was only one shot. No big deal. Two if you count the first one, he missed. But sometimes you just have a feeling about things, a hunch, and I had a feeling about this. I am a guy of faith and I believe in God and all that, but I also believe God works through practice as well. A whole lot of faith in Him and some hard work from you. And somehow, I believed that what I was seeing was the result of hard work.

Curiosity is eating me, and it won't let me go. I had to know, so I decided to dig. And I knew where to start. That evening after practice and homework, I searched for his social media page. He had to have one. Every teenager did. That's where teenagers told all of the truths of their lives, and made up the lives they wanted us to believe were true. But if I sifted through, I could find what I needed.

Found his page. Post. Pages. Pictures.

There goes Ben.

His Mom.
That must be Sam.
Art?
Music?
This guy is weird.

I kept looking. Clicking. My answer is here. And then I came across a picture with Dee holding a trophy. Date said it was a year old. I zoomed in to read the inscription. "One on One Streetball Champion"

Huh? Wait! Streetball like basketball streetball? Pictures of Dee as young as 9 in tournaments from Dyer to the city. Ribbons and medals and accolades. Trophies taller than him. I found video of him. The type with captions at the bottom and beats in the background. He was good. Unorthodox. A lefty. His shot was ugly for sure. But he must have been shooting that way for a long time because even with elbows flailing and wrist flapping the ball went through the hoop. He knew how to score. And he was quick. Man that guy was lightning quick and flashy in the school of Uncle Drew and Ruckers Park.

This guy was a street balling legend. "I knew it! I knew it! He knows how to play ball. He lied!"

Questions demand answers but answers sometimes only produce more questions. Why did he lie? Why did he not just tell us that knows how to play? Why did he not try out for the team? And why did Ben not say anything when he knew we needed players? I stormed into the gym the next day. Most of the team already there. Dee was handing out practice

What Just Happened

jerseys. I walked over and snatched them out of his hand. "Give me those. Take this." I threw the ball toward him with force. "Shoot it."

"Jon. Why?"

"Because you can. Shoot it!"

Confusion was all over Dee's face. "I don't get you dude. All the questions yesterday and now this? What is up with you man?"

"Just shoot the ball Dee. Shoot that ball right now!" He slowly walked toward the free throw line. "No. Shoot it from out here. Shoot a three like you did yesterday. Like you always do." My last sentence caught his attention. He was now staring at me and I was staring right back at him. "Shoot that ball Dee."

He dropped the ball and tried to walk away "I don't want to."

"Dee, I know who you are. I've seen the videos man. Why didn't you tell us that you hoop?" Now I was staring at Ben. "Ben why didn't you say anything?

Dad walked in and could feel the tension. "What's going on here?"

"Dee was just about to explain to us why he never told us he was a championship streetballer."

"Who? This kid? He hit one shot and now he is a champion? That was a fluke."

"No dad. That wasn't a fluke was it Dee? You actually know how to play. Question is why didn't you or Ben say anything? Are you a spy from Coastal Dee? Is that what it is?" My conclusion was borrowed from the book of dad's suspicions. But I had no other book to pull from. This was too strange. Now dad was in.

"Speak son. Do you play basketball yes or no?"

"Yes sir I do."

"So why didn't you try out, say something?"

I couldn't hold myself back. "You lied Dee. Talking all that God talk but you lied."

"No Jon. You never asked. And you never asked because you didn't spect much from a scrawny freshman like me, did ya?"

Then Ben spoke up. "I-I-I-It was because of me. I told him not to say nothing."

"Ben you don't have answer no questions," Dee said.

"Nah man. I knew this was coming. It always does. The day my mom made him come to practice I knew this would happen. I-I-I told him 'You better not tell them you play. I don't want you on my team. This is my team. My space. Not yours'. H-H-He always takes over. S-s-s-sucks up all the air and don't leave nothing for me to breathe. I'm the oldest, but no one don't never know cause he don't know how to share space, and then people always like him more than me. S-s-so I told him 'Boy you better not tell nobody.' I told him that."

"Son is that true?"

"Yes sir. I have played ball all my life. Longer than Benny. And I am good at it. Streetball at least. But this was Ben's space, his friends, and I was trying to respect that."

What Just Happened

"This is not Ben's space Dee. This is mine. And in my space if you can play, you make the team. You and Ben can work out that other stuff somewhere else. We need players and you say you can play. Now all that's left is for you to prove it. Jon, Dee get on the court. Let's go."

But Dee responded, "No thank you coach. With all due respect I don't need to prove anything to anybody sir. I agreed to be the manager, not a player, and that's all I intend to be. That is if you will still have me. This ain't about me anyway."

With that, Dee walked over to me and grabbed the jerseys I was still holding and started to hand them out to a silent team that was still shocked by what had just happened. When he was done, he said, "If there's nothing else coach, I have taken care of all of my duties and I would like to go home early today if you don't mind."

Coach was just as stunned as the rest of us. "That's fine Dee. You may go."

"Thank you, coach."

Chapter 10

YOUR CALLING

What happened next, I only know because Dee told me. And I am so glad that he did.

When Dee left the gym, he did not go home like he said he would. He ran over to The Church at the Park. He had to talk to Sam, and he knew he was probably there. He always was. Dee hopped the fence and knocked on the big old doors. Could see that the lights were on but there was no answer. He kept knocking and knocking, every knock more desperate than the one before. He needed to talk to Sam.

He heard footsteps coming. Didn't stop knocking, as though it were possible that the person could suddenly change course and decide not to open the door. Finally he heard the deadbolt unlocking and chain being removed. Through all of that Dee didn't stop knocking. In fact he never stopped till the door was open and Sam was standing in front of him. He pushed past Sam. No hello.

"What took you so long?"

"Hello to you too sir."

Your Calling

"Hello. What took you so long? I was knocking so long my knuckles are almost bloody."

"I was using the bathroom Dee and what I was doing can take a minute."

"Fiber."

"What?"

"A little more fiber in your diet would help shorten those bathroom visits by a lot and then you could answer the door quicker. Oh and water."

Sam laughed. "You fool. What do you want Dee?"

Dee headed for the front pew. Crashed into it. Laying down staring at the cobwebbed chandelier above. In a very weird way that was the place he went to when he needed to think, talk. The pew closest to the alter in the empty church sanctuary. It was so different there when there was no band, no preacher, no people. Peaceful. He could think. "They know now."

"Dee I am many things. A mind reader is not one of them. Who is they and what do they know?"

"The team knows that I play ball."

"Ok. And why is that a problem again?"

"It is a problem because I didn't want them to know. If they know then they are going to ask me to play. If they ask me to play, then I might play. And if I play then I may be good."

"And that is a problem why?"

"Because I'm done with basketball Sam. I gave that up. It's a distraction. I'm focused on looking out for that big thing God has called me to do in this world like you said. So I don't have time to be distracted by basketball. I decided that I am not playing ball no more."

Sam chuckled.

"Why are you laughing? Thought you would have been proud."

"Sorry. Yes. I am Dee. I am. I am so impressed by your focus on finding out what it is that God has called you to do. Don't know many teenagers willing to leave everything behind, especially something they love, to pursue God's call on their life. I know I wasn't that passionate about God when I was your age. So yes, I'm proud. But I want to challenge your thinking just a little bit."

"Seems as though that's all you ever do."

"Just go with me on this one. Could we say basketball is a gift? I mean I can't play and believe me I've tried."

"I guess."

"And I think we can say it is a good gift too, huh?"

"Yeah. Sure."

"Well the bible says that all good gifts come from above.[2] So I believe God gave you that gift Dee."

"Ok?"

"Do you have to break any of your life principles to play? Does it cause you to sin? Pull you away from your God commitment? Church?"

"No."

"And you love playing right?"

---

2   James 1:17

Your Calling

"I do."

"Alright. Well then it passes the smell test."

"Smell test?"

"Keep following. I'm going somewhere. I don't think that people believe that God is a good Father who loves to give good gifts Dee.[3] And so when they think about His will for their lives, they think it must be a punishment. They think that it is an automatic call to a life of misery and boringness."

"I'm not sure boringness is a word Sam."

"God never said that He called us to a life of misery. He said He came so that we could experience life at its best and I think you are at your best in the area where you are gifted.[4] Is it possible that God's purpose for your life is going to be found at the intersection of your gifts, your passions and His glory? Could God use what you are good at to build His kingdom? I told you that you needed to look for God's purpose for your life and you looked for a pulpit, a mic and a stage. But that's my purpose Dee, not yours. Is it possible that the pulpit God has for you is on the court with a basketball?"

"I guess."

"Remember what we said Dee. When you don't know what God wants you to do, keep praying and walking and do your best at what you put your hands to every day. Eventually your purpose will find you. Dee, I think your purpose has found you. God wants

---
3   Matthew 7:11
4   John 10:10

you to give Him glory on the basketball court. That's the place where He is going to use you to change the world."

Dee was sitting up now. "I guess I just thought God was calling me into the ministry."

"He is. Just not the ministry you thought He was calling you to. You have always been a great basketball player. Now you need to figure out how to be a great basketball player for God. That is your ministry. "Whatsoever your hands find to do, do it with all your might." That's Solomon. Your hands have found something to do. Now you just got to do it with all your might Dee."[5]

"Now how am I supposed to do that Sam? What exactly am I supposed to do?"

"Not sure. But if you keep walking, He will show you."

"God and these riddles man. I'm gonna need Him to be a little more direct with His communication."

Sam responded thoughtfully, "I used to think that too. Then I heard an old preacher say that if God told us where our lives were going, we would all go running in the opposite direction. So He gives us as much as we need to know, when we need to know it. What we know now is that you were called to that team. So what you do next is go to that practice and give it your absolute best. Leave the rest to God."

Then Sam put his hand on Dee's shoulder and prayed. This prayer was not like any that had come

---

[5] Ecclesiastes 9:10

before. He had always prayed that God reveal Dee's purpose to him. Now Sam prayed for Dee to accept what God had revealed. "God, may Dee's feet obediently follow where You are obviously leading, in Jesus name, amen."

Dee left the church he ran into, walking. He would need all the time he could get, to think about what Sam had just said.

For the next two practices Dee was a no show. So was Ben. What had happened was on everyone's mind, but no one spoke on it. We didn't know how to. He was our light, and that light was out, so the gym was dark again, lacking the life we had gotten used to. I didn't want to be there. No one did. Didn't want to think about the possibility of things going back to what they had been without Dee.

I found myself grieving I guess, as if he were dead or something. I was heavy. My stomach in knots. I needed to talk to someone about it. Get it off my chest. "Dad suppose he doesn't come back?"

"Who?"

"You know who I'm talking about. What if Dee does not come back? We need him!"

"If he doesn't come back, he doesn't come back."

His voice was firm and cold. That is the way he had always been. Slow to connect, quick to let go. Me? I was opposite. Once I was for you, I was for you. And somehow, though our time was new, I was really for

Dee.

"Dad he is such big part of the team. He's helped us so much. Who is gonna do all the things that he did? All the things you used to do? You do remember what it was like before Dee right? Maybe you could give him a call. Talk to his mom. She will get him to come back."

"Son if Dee does not come back the balls will still get pumped, the jerseys will get handed out, the floor will get swept, and we will move on. You get too attached to people. People are like the tide. They will come and they will go son. And you would save yourself from a lot of hurt if you would learn how to just let go and move on."

Not the first time he had said something like that to me. Think he saw my bend toward relationship as a flaw. A weakness no young man could afford. Guess he wished that I was more of a loner like him. But I saw my love for friendships as strength. A gift to my DNA from my mom maybe. It was what made life happy for me. And though I could not yet say Dee was a friend, he was definitely someone I did not want to see walk away.

But I failed to convince dad of my values. And so there was no movement. Dad refused to call and check on Dee, and Dee never called to tell us what was going on. So we were all left in the dark.

The weekend passed. Walk into the gym on Monday. It is squeaky clean. Everything is in its right

Your Calling

place. Goals are already down, and balls are already out. The curtains are open. Light is flooding in. I knew dad hadn't done that. He wouldn't have had the time. These details have someone else's fingerprints on it. I am starting to get excited. I am hoping that my heart is right. And then out of the locker room door Dee came walking and he was doing what he had always done. Pumping balls and laying out uniforms as if he had never left. I was so relieved. I ran over and hugged him. I am hugging him. What was I thinking?

"Whoa there partner. Hugging is not a part of my contract." We laughed.

I told him that I was sorry about the questions. And calling him a liar. And questioning his faith. There was not excuse for it. "I was just so confused man. If I could, if I was half as good as you are I would.... But there is no good excuse. There is just no good reason for me to treat you this way. I am really sorry man. And then I didn't see you at practice. I thought you quit, and it was all because of me."

"Dude chill. I took the day off on Thursday and had a dentist appointment on Friday. I may be a lot of things but I'm no quitter. You did annoy me though. At some point I wanted to give you a big momma sized whooping, but God used you, so I'll spare you." We laughed.

Dee walked over to the middle of the court and called for all the guys to gather round. Coach stood off on the side. Close enough to hear, far enough to fake disinterest. "I want to apologize to you all for being a distraction in that last practice. You too coach. This team has a lot to achieve so there is no room for distractions. That will never happen again. I also want to apologize for not being upfront with you about who I am. Guess there are some things about me that still need a lot of work. That's on me. If y'all would still have me, I would like to continue my role as manager. And coach if you would have me, I would also like to see if I can be a part of this team... as a player, a part of beating Coastal."

I spoke up. "Dee you are already a part of our team and we would have hunted you down if you ever thought about leaving."

Coach interrupted my celebration, "Hey Jon. Think that's my role son. Dee now it's gonna be a lot of work to do both."

"I know sir."

"I'm gonna need you to get here a little earlier."

"Yes sir."

"And I am not going to go easy on you. You'll still have to do all the stuff you had to do before. No excuses."

"I'm allergic."

"Allergic to what Dee?"

"Excuses." Dee smiled. Dad just squinted his eyes.

"And on playing for me? You're gonna have to earn a place on this team just like every other player did son. You're not gonna just walk in here and tell me you're on my team. This ain't charity. You got to show

Your Calling

me you deserve a spot. I don't care how many likes you got on those street ball videos."

"I wouldn't have it any other way coach."

"Ok. Alright. If you are good with all of that, let's put you through a workout and see how it goes."

The workout must have gone pretty well cause by the next practice Dee was in uniform. With his manager stuff, he had not skipped a beat. As usual he had paid attention to every possible detail. The balls and goals were still out, uniforms prepped, curtains drawn, and the gym freshly swept. "Hey Jon, I put an something special in the water today. Let me know if it gives your workout a little extra boost."

"Something legal I hope?"

"Hope so. Ordered it from Wal-Mart." We laughed. Those thoughtful details. The only thing missing was his now famous managers jacket.

On the court he was wild. Raw. Intense. On defense he flew around the court like tornado in Kansas. It was an energy I had never seen. Hands waving. Noise making. Shoes squeaking. But he was the same Dee that walked into the gym that day. Always talking. The mere distraction was enough to make the guy he was guarding drop the ball. "Dan you on him like peanut butter on jelly. Yup"

"Izzie wave them hands like you in church and the praise is good."

"Yo Ben! You got a mouse in the house!"

I Am Jon

"Jon you put him skates dude."

"Make em feel you boys."

The talking was consistently constant. Never ending. Not even a pause. He talked to his teammates. He talked to himself. He talked to the ball. Coach liked when his players communicated on the court but even Dee talked coach crazy. "Dee are you ever quiet."

"Nope. If I'm on the court and I ain't talking check my pulse. I might be dead." But talking wasn't all he did on the court. There were flashes of brilliance. The ability to see plays none of us saw. The audacity to try things that none of us dare try. He had a loud confidence, without even a whisper of arrogance. A special talent that even a blind man could see.

But all that talent and brilliance was raw and wild. Not tamed enough to play with 5. Not contained enough to give it a position on the court, for it had no regard for position, and no respect for boundaries. Dee was free and we needed his freedom, creativity. But we hadn't had enough time to figure out how to use it. It was already the middle of the season, and just two days before our next league game. Not nearly enough time for him to be ready to play. Coach pulled all of us together at the end of practice to talk about the game plan.

"Let's put our hands together for our newest Providence Lion, Dee. Boy! All that flying around out there is great. Still fouling a lot, and talking way too much, but I like that energy and the effort."

Your Calling

"Go Dee."

"Dee this is a gonna be a really tough game on the road against Newport, and we really need this win."

"Yes sir coach. We lost to them last year and they have pretty much the same team. And it is a road game in a really tough environment. Heard their fans are vicious. Uncouth! Call you all kinds of names your momma didn't name ya."

Coach continued, "I'm gonna have you suit up, but you probably won't see any playing time for this one. You're just not ready for it, and I don't want to set you or the team up to fail."

There was not a hint of surprise in him. "Didn't expect to coach."

"And you are ok with that?"

"Coach it is an honor to finally get to wear that Providence jersey. This practice gear is cool, but to put on the actual Providence purple uniform and be a Lion is a dream. Plus, there are a lot of ways to be a good teammate. So no matter if I ever get off of the bench, you are going to feel me on the court." That little window opened the door and Dee took over the huddle. "Boys we are gonna win this game. We are gonna win this game. I guarantee it. Ask me how I know."

"How you know Dee?"

"Because we believe. We will win because we believe we will win. Any doubt in your mind, any fear on your heart, chuck it. Tell it bye bye. Replace fear with faith and believe. Bible says when you believe you can tell mountains to move and they must move.[6] We got a mountain that needs to get out of our way. But if we believe in us, nothing can stop us." Then Dee pushed his little scrawny body through the bodies to the middle of the huddle and shouted. "Providence repeat after me. We believe!"

"We believe!"
"We believe!"
"We believe!"
"We believe!"
"Ahhhhhhhhhh!"

---

6   Mark 11:23

Newport High

1 SAMUEL 18
3-4 *Jonathan, out of his deep love for David, made a covenant with him. He formalized it with solemn gifts: his own royal robe and weapons—armor, sword, bow, and belt.*

Chapter 11

NEWPORT HIGH

Thursday, January 20th. Away game at Newport. Don't know if anybody remembered that chant. If they did, it did not show.

We got off the bus and a few of their fans were already waiting for us, shouting. I couldn't hear the things they were saying. Thank God for the gift of a good pair of noise canceling headphones. I was sure that whatever they were saying were not words of encouragement and welcome. Once the game started the crowd was louder than we expected, and their players were better than they were the last time we saw them. Nothing worked for us. Everything went in for them. We were already down by 15 points at the half.

At half time dad screamed words at us. Not unusual. After a while his screaming always became a loud blur none of us heard. It communicated nothing. Before the bullhorn talk was over, it was time to go back on to the court. He dropped the clipboard and marched out of the locker room leaving us even less motivated than we were when we walked off of the floor. We were slowly rising, seemingly resistant to returning to the punishment of the game. Something had to change.

Dee walked over to me, "Jon you are our leader. Lead!"

"I don't know what to say Dee. We are getting smoked out there."

"Jon, we need you to be our inspiration. You can't lose hope. If you don't believe we can win, we won't believe we can win. So I need you to suck it up and say something."

"Something like what Dee? What can I say? I've been the motivator for this team all season and I am just empty. For once I just don't know what to say."

"Good. Cause now you can get out of the way and let God speak. He has something that He has wanted to say, and He needed you to come to the end of your words so that He could speak. God will tell you what to say. You just got to be brave enough to say it. Lead us Jon."

"Pray for me Dee." I got up and stood in front of our wounded crew.

"Are we having fun yet?" Nervous laugh. "Cause I'm not. Actually nothing about this season has been fun. Nothing! Not practice. Not games. Nothing. And nothing has been easy. Seems like a task to just get out there on the court, far less win a game."

"You are *not* lying," said Ash.

"Well I don't want to play anymore. Not if it means that I have to feel like this all the time. Basketball is supposed to be fun. Right now it feels like a curse. So I'm done." I sat on the bench behind me. Started to take off my jersey and unlace my shoes. They are staring at me mouths wide open. I had taken off my jersey and stuffed it in my bag before anybody said a word.

"Jon, you serious? You just gonna quit on us? Right in the middle of the game?"

"We quit on ourselves before this game even began Dan! From the minute we walked off the bus we acted as though we were gonna lose this game. And then we went out on the court and did everything we could to prove we were right. So all I'm doing is following through on what we started. I am picking up my bag heading for the door."

"This ain't right Jon. You can't just up and leave. We can't go down like this." Every player to a man looked at me with the eyes of an abandoned child.

"You know what? Y'all are right! This ain't right," I said turning around. "And no we can't go down like this. So somebody tell me we won't let it happen. Somebody tell me that we are going to go back out there and fight. That we are going to get back to having fun. Playing Providence basketball. Somebody make me put my jersey back on. Make me a believer!"

Ben spoke up. "Y-y-you know guys I-I know I ain't the best basketball player. I just ain't. I'm tall and y'all needed a tall dude. But I ain't that great out there. B-but you know what. I know I'm better than what

Newport High

I been showing. I'm gonna go out there and give it my best. I promise you that Jon."

"Thanks Benny."

"Me too."

"I'm down."

One after the next, each player to a man made a commitment to give their best. And that is all I ever really wanted. Cause just like Pops used to say, "when you done gave your best not even angels could do better."

"Now Dee, doesn't look like you are gonna get into this game bro. But that doesn't mean we don't need you. We need you to keep your word and bring the heat bro. We need to hear you. And we're gonna need your best."

"Jon you can count on me."

"Alright. Looks like we are ready to get back out there. Dee, we need something to say. Give us something."

"I know how to do that real good. Boys repeat after me. We will."

"We will."

"Win"

"Win."

"We will"

"We Will."

"Win."

"Win."

"We can't be stopped."

"We can't be stopped."

"We won't be stopped."

"We won't be stopped."

"Ahhhhhhhhhhhhh."

"Now put your joy shoes on and get out there and break a leg." Stares. "Ohhhh. Guess that might not have been the best thing to say." We roared.

Coach came back towards the locker room annoyed, wondering what had taken us so long to get out to the court. "What were you guys doing in there. The ref was about to call the game."

"We were putting our joy shoes on." Confused. Even more annoyed.

The team that walked back onto that court was most definitely not the one that coach left in that locker room, or the one that was getting handled the half before. We had a bounce in our step. Confidence in our eyes. I could no longer hear the crowd. Their insults faded to black. We walked like warriors ready to fight. Score 37-22.

Third quarter. Dee still has not played. But I don't think he knows. He is too busy keeping his word, cause even from the bench we felt him on the court.

"Lock them up boys."

"Nothing easy Izzie. Nothing easy". End of the third. Score 41-31.

We scrapped. We fought. Pounced on loose balls like hungry dogs on a bone. The whole time the bullhorn on the bench was never silent. Not for a moment.

"Make em work boys. Make em work."

"It's a block party."

"Benny you are the King of that key. Rule bro. Rule." Score 46-40

For me Dee's words were my fuel. I loved every minute of his talking and taunting. And somehow, I found a gear I had never found before. All of a sudden, the basket looked as big as the ocean and once I got going, I could not be stopped. The team saw it. They felt it. And they kept feeding me the ball.

Crossover. Lay up. Good.

Rainbow shot in the paint. Good

Even step back three. Hand in face. Good.

They kept feeding me and I keep eating. And the better I played the more Dee talked. "Get that change Jon. Cha Cha Ching!"

The gym is as silent as a church at communion. Dee's one voice dominated, literally subduing an entire crowd. If Newport had really thought it through, they would have gagged him and taped his mouth closed because his words were our fuel. The louder he shouted, the harder we played. "Come on boys. This is it. The mountain is moving. The mountain is moving. Believe boys believe." Score 48-48.

Dee jumped up off the Bench and started to throw his body around. Coach screamed, "Dee what are you doing?"

"Orange Justice coach! It's a dance. Don't worry, I'll teach you after the game."

Rebound. Fastbreak. Layup. Score 50-48.

We took the lead with 3 minutes to go and never

I Am Jon

looked back. "Jon one more rebound to a triple double. Go get it bro." Ben took a shot. Off of the back iron. Ball is in the air. It is gonna be mine. Get out of my way. Snatch it out of the air. Triple double done. It was my first.

Buzzer sounded. The gym was stunned. Final score was 59- 50. I finished with 13 points and 11 assist 10 rebounds. Coach was true to his word. Dee never got into the game. But he was also never not in it. Never subbed. Never took a timeout. His cheering literally never stopped.

At the end of the game back in the locker room coach walked into the center of the room, "In all my years of coaching I have literally never seen anything like what I saw tonight. I just can't explain it. Y'all came out of that locker room at halftime like warriors. Would not be denied. Great job. I am so proud to say that tonight's game ball goes to the leader on the court, our captain, my son, Jon. Great job son."

The pride on his face was beyond full. But I could not receive that ball. "Thanks dad. But I was not the real MVP tonight. Every one of you guys who were in that locker room or out there on that court know who the real MVP tonight was. I don't think this has ever happened before, maybe in the history of sports. But the most important player tonight did not play a single minute. The real MVP." Then I walked over and put game ball in Dee's hands, and we all mobbed him.

BROTHERS

The bus ride home...crazy. The boys were loud and hyped. Understandably so. We sat in the sauce of our win, telling and retelling the story of the game, hyperbole building its legend brick by brick. Each player replayed the other's highlight reel in turn. "Remember when..." and "did you see..." thrown around like confetti. They were having so much fun.

   I sat in my usual seat, left side, kind of middle of the bus. All the action had migrated to the back. I was cool with that. I was happy too, but somehow tonight my happiness made me think not talk.

   "I am so happy to see them happy."

   "I wish I could bottle this up and save it."

   "That win was so improbable."

   Shoot. I forgot to text Michal. I usually shot her a text soon after every game, win or loss. But with all the excitement I guess I just forgot. "Hey, forgot to text you after the game."

   "YEAH YOU DID. Had me over here sweating but YRG. It's all over IG."

   "Already? SMH"

   "ROTF. When you don't come thru, I got other sources LOL."

   "SRY"

   "NP. Heard you had a monster game."

   "The TEAM played well."

   "Exactly what I thought you would say. Did Dee play?"

I Am Jon

"No. Yes. Kinda. All of the above.

"Huh."

"Dee did not play but he was the reason we won."

"?"

"Hard to explain by text. Come by the house later. We have to work on the history project."

Her next answer was swift. "You mean the one that's due tomorrow? The one I told you we should have started last week? RME."

"Just come."

We got back to town later than I thought we would have. A lot later. An accident on the highway had drivers craning their necks to look. As a result we were held hostage by the traffic for an hour. But on the bus no one complained about the long ride. They probably didn't even notice. They were too busy being happy. And joy has a way of making time go faster. When we finally pulled into the school driveway none of the guys stuck around. Probably all rushed home to tell the story of the night again to an anxiously awaiting audience.

I got off the bus and walked into the locker room. Just sat there. Still thinking about the game. Still lost in my thoughts. I thought briefly about all the losing we had done and wondered if that game that night could strike a turn for our season. The sound of someone walking in shook me from my thoughts. It was Dee. What was he doing here? I completely forgot that there were still things that had to be done. In spite of our thrilling win, we still had practice the next day. Someone had to prepare for it, and unfortunately that someone was Dee. He came in without saying a word, took off his uniform and put on his managers jacket. Made me sad to see him wearing that jacket again. The rest of us got to enjoy that evening without pause. His was interrupted by the responsibilities that jacket brought. Ball bags still had to go back to the locker room. Jerseys had to be thrown into the washing machine. Floor still had to be swept. Coolers cleaned.

    I was tired. But so was he. And couldn't feel good about going home leaving one of my teammates stuck with all the work. "Sorry that you have do all this work man. You should just go home and leave it till tomorrow. This is small stuff. No one will even notice."

    "I know no one notices Jon. But I notice. And that's enough."

    I felt foolish. Like I had insulted him. "Sorry man. Didn't mean that we don't appreciate what you do. Just thought that it would be nice for you to go home like all the other guys."

    "It's cool. I know that most of the team doesn't notice the small stuff I do. But that is the way it is supposed to be. The better I do the small things the less you ever have to think about them."

    "I guess. But doesn't it ever bother you? That you get stuck doing all of this."

    "I don't get stuck doing anything. I chose to do this. No one made me. And I take pride in what I do. Makes me feel good on the inside when I know that I have done a good job. My best. So I really don't need lights, or the mic or a trophy with my name. No one has to know except me and God."

"Man, God don't care about how you sweep a floor. He got a lot of other important stuff to worry about."

"But I think He does care about how I sweep the floor Jon. When I work hard it honors him. I think He looks at how I handle the small stuff, so He knows if I am ready for bigger things.[7] Everything I do, I need to do it as though I am doing it for God. At least that's what Sam said."

"That guy Sam."

"Plus, feels good to do things for others. Even if they never acknowledge it."

That last statement left me feeling selfish, lazy. My hands reached for a broom on their own and I started to sweep beside him. We were tired but company made work enjoyable. Honest. Short. Almost seemed as though we didn't have enough time to talk. When we got done, we headed into the locker room one last time. I still hadn't put my bag in my locker. I saw Dee pack his gym bag with his sneakers and his ball and sling it over his shoulder. "What are you doing?"

The look on Dee's face was one half sarcastic and the other half annoyedly confused. "Um, getting my stuff?"

"I can see that Dee! Why don't you leave that stuff in your locker? It's a chore to have to bring two bags

---

[7] Matthew 25:23

to school every day."

"Your dad never gave me a locker. Said there were none left."

I was livid. If there was anybody on this team who deserved to have a locker it was him. "That's not fair! Every player on our team has a locker. And you are as much a player on this team as I am. You take my locker." I immediately turned around and started to empty the locker of my stuff, ignoring whatever he would say about my offer.

"I can't do that. You got the corner locker and there's not a player on this team that wouldn't kill to have it. That spot is always reserved for the captain of the team and you waited a long time and worked really hard for that. You earned it. I can't take it."

"You are right. I worked hard to get that locker and I earned the right to have it. But I also earned the right to give it away if I want and I chose to give it to you. So as captain I am telling you that I want you to have it and you haven't earned the right to say no. Plus, I could put my stuff in my dad's office. He won't even notice the smell cause everything in there stinks anyway."

He was just standing there. I walked over and took his bag from his hand, put it in the locker and gave him the key.

"Jon I'm not used to this."

"Used to what?"

"Being thought about. I am always the guy who

I Am Jon

thinks about others. No one ever thinks about me."

"Well that needs to change. You are now our brother and you will never be forgotten as long as I am around. Never! I see something in you Dee. Something absolutely amazing. And I would bet anything that Providence High and all of Dyer is going to see what I see really soon. I guarantee it. That's exactly what I told my friend Michal."

As soon as her name left my mouth a thought punched me in the head. History project. Michal waiting, for hours. I'm in so much trouble. "I gotta go."

I shot out of that gym like bees were chasing me and ran the whole way home. One full mile at top speed. Don't think I walked even once. By the time I got home she was gone. Check my phone. She had left 2 voicemails and 3 text. "Michal so sorry. OMW."

"I waited for 2 hours for you sir CWOT. You better get your part of the project done. I don't care if it takes you all night."

Didn't bother to respond. Was too scared to. But I did get it done. And it did take all night.

Not Your Style

1 SAMUEL 17

38-39 *Then Saul dressed David in his own tunic. He put a coat of armor on him and a bronze helmet on his head. David fastened on his sword over the tunic and tried walking around, because he was not used to them. "I cannot go in these," he said to Saul, "because I am not used to them." So he took them off.*

Chapter 12

NOT YOUR STYLE

By the time we got to school on Friday all anyone was talking about was the Newport game. The privileged few who had actually been there were giving personal accounts like embedded reporters back from the war. I got to school early. Wasn't normal for me. Walked up the stairs through the main doors and down the hall toward my locker. Can't tell you how many people stopped me. High fived me. Fist pumped me. Even Stanley Foster, a guy who made bullying his chosen career, stopped to ask me questions about the game. "Good job Taylor. Made me proud." And we don't even talk like that.

The principle addressed it during morning announcements over the intercom. Could tell he was giddy. "We are so very very proud of our boys for the way they represented our school on last night. I have already gotten a call from the local newspaper asking for my comments on this historic win. You can read the article in tomorrow's daily news. Front page."

Don't know that it was all that historic. But it was a legit win over a legit team. Easily the biggest win we had all season. Maybe for the past two seasons. The Principle had all the members of the team stand in their classes and asked the class to applaud us. We walked into the cafeteria together for lunch, like we always did during the season. The room exploded in applause and a raucous "We are Providence" chant. I got chills. Cafeteria workers told us that lunch was going to be free for us that day. I felt like a rock star. Guess when you have been bad for as long as we have, being mediocre is like being really good.

Everybody in Dyer was finally talking about basketball. Everyone was feeling good. Everyone, except dad. "Ok, so we got a good win the other night. Everyone is talking about it. Good. But now it's going to your head. You guys are practicing like you won a championship or something. Where is the trophy? Somebody show me the trophy we won for beating Newport. Should we throw a parade? Is a free cafeteria lunch all you play for? Let them celebrate. We work. Beating Newport was not the goal. Beating Coastal is. So stop feeling yourselves and start prepping for our next game. Yesterday's win is yesterday's news."

He was right. We had to get that win out of our heads and get back to work. That Newport game hadn't come easy and nor without cost. Simon was hurt, again. And this time it looked like he would actually miss some games. He was our backup point guard. He played at least 10 minutes a game, sometimes more. Someone would have to step up and take his place.

Not sure that all the players got what coach said. But one person who seemed to take the message to heart was Dee. He had done what he had to do from the bench at Newport, but I knew that was not where he wanted to stay. He wasn't just going to be the uniform wearing fan for the whole season. He had made this team for a reason and with Simon hurt we needed him on the court. Not on the bench. So he worked harder and differently. He did less talking and more listening. He asked me to explain plays and then went home and studied them and came back the next day asking for more. He was sponge and there didn't seem to be anything we could do saturate him. He was determined to earn his minutes on the court. Prove his worth. And he was. But dad still hadn't put him in the game.

"Jon, what am I doing wrong? It's been 3 games and I have not even smelled the court. Even when we need a point guard out there, coach never even looks my way. He put Izzie out there to play point last game Jon. Izzie! He wouldn't pass a ball if you paid him. This just don't make no sense."

I couldn't help. Didn't make sense to me either. Told him that from where I was standing, he was doing all the right things. "You should talk to coach. He is reasonable."

"I could use a lot of different words to describe your dad. I don't think that anybody including you thinks he's reasonable."

Not Your Style

"You just have to get to know him. He really does have a big heart."

I really did believe that. When it came to dad, I was a constant optimist. Couldn't help it. Wasn't blind to his weaknesses. I cringed sometimes in practice hearing him scream at the players. Wondered how he kept his job the way he spoke to the other staff. Found myself constantly making excuses for him. Trying to prove that he was not as bad as people said he was. I knew they were excuses. But he was my dad and I had also seen the depth of good in him and that good was amazing. I remained hopeful his good would become his norm so that everybody could see what I saw and love the man that I loved. But to this point, that seemed to be a lost cause. "I'm sure he will at least hear you out."

"Well I sure do hope so, cause I could see this conversation going all kinda wrong." He was right. The conversation could go wrong quickly and not even I could tell him how to avoid that happening. Took a few days but Dee eventually took my advice. He waited till the end of the practice when all the other guys had left and took his chance.

"Coach can I have a second?" Dad didn't even lift his head.

"I am grateful for the shot you gave me to make the team. I remember that you said that I had to earn my time on the court, and I have been working hard for the last few weeks. But you have still never called my number. Is there something I am doing wrong?'

"No."

"Is there something you want out there that I am not giving in practice?"

"Nope. You work hard."

"So coach if you don't mind can you tell me what I am doing wrong?"

"I don't like your style. I'm not for that streetball cross over stuff. Honestly, I think it disrespectful to call that stuff basketball cause it's not. I like fundamentals. I like my basketball plain without icing. Not all that new fangle dangle showboating. Showboating is for stars and we don't need stars on this team Dee. We need guys that just come in and do their jobs."

"Ok. So exactly what part of my style would you like me to change coach? I am willing to work on it."

"Dee to be a real basketball player you have got to master the fundamentals. And the most basic of all of them is that this is a team sport. Streetball can't teach you that. So all of it. You need to get rid of all of it and start over so that you can be on level with the other guys. You need to strip your game down and start over son. That streetball stuff only works against kids that don't really know how to play the game. But we play against the best players in the state."

That stung. Real basketball player? Dee stood there for a moment. Thought about taking that one on the chin and just walking away. But he couldn't. "Coach I respectfully disagree. Basketball is a simple

Not Your Style

game. Nobody cares what your style is. I've played some of these "real" basketball players you're talking about. In the summer they all come out to streetball tournaments. Trevor Cook from Greenland. Brian Dorsey from Kirkwood. Miles Patterson from Stanton. Some of the best in-coming freshmen last year. All great players. I'm not the boasting type but I beat every single one of them...with my style."

"Dee I'm gonna put it to you simple. This is my team. And if you want to play on my team you will have to learn how to play my way."

"Yes sir coach."

When Dee told me what coach said I felt bad for putting him up to have that talk with him. I could see that the conversation had taken something out of him. Some of his shine had faded and I could understand why. Honestly, I would have been crushed. Probably quit. But I knew that I couldn't let him do that. There was too much in him to allow anyone's words, even the coach, to discourage him.

"Dee both you and I know that you are an amazing basketball player. You would have to be blind not to see it. My dad just doesn't see it yet, but he will."

"Your dad wants me to completely change the way I play. But that is not my style Jon. I would be lost if I tried to be somebody else out there."

"Yes and we would all lose because that is not you. You are not me or Izzie or Ben or Dan. You are you. And we need you to be you. You are unique Dee. God made you that way. And you have to be yourself." I could see his spirit lifting. He had encouraged me in the past and now it was my turn to encourage him. "Stuff like this can shake your confidence man. Don't let that happen Dee. You have got to use this to get stronger. Be more determined. You got to keep believing in yourself. Keep preparing. You told me that God cares about how you sweep the floor. And He is..."

"Preparing me for bigger things. Didn't think you were really listening."

"Well I was. And I know God is gonna honor your hard work. Your time will come. I believe that! When it does you just gotta be ready."

Still Talking

1 SAMUEL 31
8-10 *The next day, the Philistines found Saul and his three sons dead on Mount Gilboa. They displayed his armor in the shrine of the Ashtoreth. They nailed his corpse to the wall at Beth Shan.*

Chapter 13

STILL TALKING

It had been a pretty miserable winter. Wet and cold and gray seemingly every other day. Every morning the trees and roofs were frosted. Thick fog covered the apple orchards. Cold made my breath turn to smoke. By the evening the frost was gone only to be replaced by miserable rain. I didn't mind the morning cold so much, but I hated the rain. I had lived through many Dyer winters without bothering to buy a coat or an umbrella. This year I had to get both.

With weather like that, about the only thing for anyone round here to look forward to in the fall was basketball. Before the season started there was a late summer buzz at the barber shop discussing the new kid on the team. Discounts at the pizza store, free soda at the corner store. The Dyer newspaper always did a feature story. Ran it on the front page with one of those pictures that made us all look larger than life. Dad would do a few radio interviews and give all the reasons why this year was going to be different than the last. Every year the season started

Still Talking

with full gyms, roaring fans and cheerleaders for the first two, maybe three games. Seemed like the focus of the entire town was on that was happening in that gym at the beginning of the season.

But all that stuff disappeared as quickly as the morning fog. It left us with painful months of drudgery, wishing that the torture of another losing season would quickly end. By the time we would get to the Coastal rivalry game in late February it wasn't ever much of a rivalry, or much of a game. We crawled in bleeding prey, and those savage predators tore us limb from limb, and left our bones for the vultures to enjoy. Graphic? I know. But that is exactly how those games felt.

Last year's game was in our gym. The few Providence fans that bothered to show up were overrun by ravenous hoards in Coastal blue. We got killed by 25. At the end of the game their team and their fans stormed the floor and celebrated on our logo at mid court. They knew what they were doing was disrespectful, lacking any class or sportsmanship. That was their intent. I was so angry but there were so many of them that there was nothing I could do to stop it.

All those years. All those lop-sided losses. The disrespect. But I refused to hang my head. I was Providence born. Providence bread. Providence proud. My mom and dad went to this school. My grandfather and his father. No matter what our record was I would never be ashamed of Providence. Fact.

I wore my purple Providence hoodie even through abusive summer heat and shame filled stares. Wore that thing till there were holes in the pits and dad just threw it away.

But this year it was late January, and hope was strangely still with us. We were one game above .500, with a chance to make state playoffs, albeit slim. But a slim chance was a welcomed replacement for no chance at all. People around town were still talking about us. Wouldn't say the talk was all that loud, but they were talking and that was a good thing.

THE POSTER

"Newspaper came by the school again today. That's the fourth time this season."

"Well that's what happens when you ain't losing all the time." Michal was never one to go easy on us, though I knew she meant well. She was honest. But that honesty sometimes cut pretty deep. So I sometimes had to delay talking to her after a loss, till I was ready.

"Think they are just getting everyone hyped up for the big game and it's still a few weeks away."

"Ya think? Did you see this? This was from yesterday. Knew you must not have, or you would've called me." She unfolded a page from the newspaper that she had in her back pocket.

My eyes were quickly scanning the paper. Didn't quite know what I was looking at, but the title of

Still Talking

the article caught my eye. "Next!". Michal answered my face's puzzled look. "Apparently Coastal has a tradition of putting a poster up of their next opponent on a wall in their locker room. They kinda mess with it a little you know? It's like a joke. Motivation."

"Okay?" I was still puzzled. The poster thing was nothing new. We had all heard the rumors.

"Jon the article says they've had poster up of Providence since the Newport game. They have not even bothered with their other opponents. Caleb told me that the poster they have is not of the whole team."

"Forgot Caleb plays for Coastal now." Still didn't understand why she was making such a big deal of a poster.

"Not anymore. He quit."

"Whoa. Wait. Caleb quit the team?"

"Yup. Said he couldn't play on a team that would do that to his friend. In fact, he wants to tell us everything they have planned for us."

Caleb quit the team in his senior year? He is willing to be our spy? "Michal you are dragging this drama out too long. Hurry up and say what you got to say!"

My urgency moved the conversation from silly to serious faster than Michal could find her footing. All of a sudden, she found herself knee deep in a situation that she wasn't ready for. Now she had to find a way to navigate thru the door she had opened. "Jon the poster is a picture of you and your dad and what they did to it wasn't funny at all. It's just wrong."

My eyes were on the paper. I could feel my insides starting to boil. She could see it. Her speech slowed. "They stuck the poster on a wall, and they put a bullseye on it Jon. And they cut out your heads. And then their coach let them all write all over it. The things they wrote weren't kind Jon. Stuff I could never even repeat. Caleb texted me a picture of it. He wanted us to see it before he quit the team. Said he couldn't play on a team that would do that to his friend. Do you want to see it?"

No answer. Had never in all my life felt so disrespected. Not when Stanley Foster slapped my books out of my hand in the hallway. Not when some dude called me a kid when I tried to get in on a pick-up game at the park. Not even when Coastal mobbed our floor and jumped on our logo. None of that bothered me like this. To be honest what got to me was not what they did to me. It was that they had disrespected my dad.

"Jon, you ok?"

"No. I'm not ok. I am not ok! They took a picture of my dad and cut his head out ? And wrote stuff on it? And mocked him? What? Did you think I would be ok with that? Would you have been ok if they had done that to your dad?" I was screaming an avalanche of questions. Michal doesn't deserve this. She didn't do anything wrong. I know it. But she has always made room for me to express my feelings. And today angry was how I felt. "Had they done it to me I could laugh it off as some stupid joke. But

Still Talking

they did it to my dad, and that absolutely crossed the line."

"You're right."

"I'm so angry Michal. Way past angry. That's not basketball. This has nothing to do with basketball."

"That's true."

"I promise you Michal. I'm gonna crush Coastal. And when we are done, I'm gonna walk into that locker room and take that poster down myself."

Michal climbed off of the two word ledge she had been standing on for shelter from my anger. "Jon you have a right to be angry. But someone once told me 'anger is only one letter short of danger.' Keep your head on bro. You got work to do."

"Thanks sis. I can always trust you to keep me on the level."

I Am Jon

Chapter 14

WHIPLASH

I couldn't bring myself to tell dad about the poster. I didn't want him to be as distracted as I was because there were still a few games between us and Coastal. But from that day forward thoughts of beating Coastal consumed me, I guess the way they had dad. I finally understood what he had been going through and it wasn't easy.

   I pushed myself harder in practice and I pushed everyone around me just as hard. Probably too hard.

   "Ben you've got to get that rebound!"

   "Izzie was in the w-w-way. I tried."

   "You got to start doing more than just trying Ben!" Every game for the last two seasons you been trying. You've got to start producing dude. You got all that height. Do something with it! And pick your head up man. I ain't on the floor."

   "Jon I-I tried man."

   "You call that trying Ben? I call that plain lazy. You are a lazy player man."

   Dan had heard enough. "Hey Jon, you need to chill bro."

Whiplash

"Chill Dan? You think Coastal is chilling? Let's all just chill and then let's see what happens in a few weeks. Think that's a good plan?"

"Probably not. But what I do know is that you barking at Ben, at all of us really, isn't gonna do much to help us win that game. You are our leader. Don't let the pressure get to you."

Was about to bark something smart back at Dan. Wanted to tell him that I could talk to Ben however I wanted to talk to Ben. Fact there was a part of me that wanted to be pushed over the edge that day, just so I could really take all this anger out on someone, and just get these bad feelings out of me. But Dan just stood there, between Ben and me. Silent. Equally defending Ben and protecting me. And his face had this 'I know you and this isn't you' look on it. That look snatched the bite out of me. These were not my enemies. They were my brothers with whom I had fought many battles.

"I feel so much pressure to get this win guys. Sometimes I feel as though it is my job to go out there on that court and get us that win. I gotta do it. But I forget that I am not the only guy here who feels pressure. Y'all probably feeling it too huh?"

Dee said "Everyday! You not the only one who reads the newspapers or gets text from Caleb you know!"

"Y'all all knew about that?"

"Of course we know. We all know. Pretty sure every man on this team knew before you did."

I Am Jon

"Why didn't you tell me?"

"Because we all kinda knew you would be as mad as a polar bear in August. And you should be. That's normal. And human. But you got to be careful with that anger my friend. My momma used to say a fool feels anger and raises his fist. A wise man feels anger and raises a sail. It's up to you. Either way we got you."

"A polar bear in August?"

"Was either that or a mudless pig. Personally I thought the polar bear thing was a better choice." We hollered.

"For sure Dee. For sure. Ben, man I'm really sorry."

"I-Its cool Jon. You have held us d-down t-too many times to remember. W-w-we got you now. And to t-tell you the truth I-I probably should've got that rebound. I'll work harder."

"Thanks big man."

I eventually managed to stop shouting at the boys, though sometimes I had to bite planet sized holes through my tongue and pray never ending prayers in order to do it. I remembered deeply hating the way I felt the morning after, and I never wanted to feel that again. Never wanted Dan to have to be the dam to stand between the flood of my unjustified fury and the team. So I bit down hard and prayed even harder. Whenever something slipped, my brothers were patient. A glance my way was enough to tell me that I was two steps away from a deathly cliff and I was wise enough to step back. Think they

Whiplash

could see that I was trying my best and that had always been enough for them. My guys.

However what never slowed was my drive to beat Coastal. Was still the first thing I thought about when eyes cracked in the morning and the last thought to tuck me into bed at night. The poster fiasco opened a door that could only be closed by victory over the enemy. So shouting and berating was for the most part gone, only to be replaced by another voice with the same intent.

"I like the hustle boys. Like that hustle."

"Coach that was an awesome practice. You really made us work."

"Ben you are doing it big fella. Great work." I was throwing out good jobs like confetti.

Dee walked over Ben's way. "Ben you ok? You must be injured. Your neck hurting?"

Ben was Mr. Confused. "Why? I-I'm fine. I mean I think I'm fine."

"You sure?"

"I-I think so. Why you asking? Does it look like something is wrong with my neck?"

Dee walked up to his brother and got high on his tip toes so he could see. Ran his fingers across the back of his neck inspecting it with a very serious look on his face "Nope. Looks fine to me. Was just checking to see if after yesterday, all this encouragement from Jon is giving you the whiplash it is giving me." We bawled.

"Dee, you know I got it from you right?" I said.

"No sir. You've gone far beyond any example I ever gave. You are leading us by your own example Jon. We are proud to follow you." Hearing that from him was healing and good.

Think some of all the good vibes rubbed off on Dad too. Practice ran a little longer than normal. After free-throw drill, he had us all sit in the center circle of the floor. "State playoffs are still in our sights boys," he said pacing the floor in front of us, hands behind his back, eyes looking forward. "We just need wins in these last two games, and I think we can do it." He stopped pacing and looked us in our eyes. "This is the first time in a long time, really since I've been coach. That's been hard for me. All the losing ya know. Been really really hard. I watch other coaches get awards and stuff. But never me. Hearing the whispers every year. All the negativity and expectation can change you till you don't even recognize yourself. But just having a chance at success means everything. It validates years of hard work. Finally people will notice, and it is because of you. So thank you. You will never know what this means."

The vulnerability in this moment slowed the planets and melted the sun. Don't know the last time I had heard dad talk like this. It's the dad I knew was in there. The one I want everyone to know.

"I need all of you to be ready. We are going to need every single one of you guys if we are going to do this. When one man falls its got to be next man up. Now bring it in." We huddled hand on hand, and in that moment, we were one.

I took a long slow walk home, just thinking. Had a lot to think about. So much had happened over the season, really over the last two days. So much change around me, in me. Don't know that I had taken time to process it all. When I got home the lights were still on. Dad was not crashed in the couch or holed up to his room. I could see through the kitchen window that he was sitting at the kitchen table as if he was waiting to talk to me. Normally I would have had to think about why he would have been sitting there, waiting for me. But today I knew exactly why. He was nervous. And at his most nervous moments I became his Michal.

I used to think that what he wanted was conversation. So I would come in with comment gun loaded and mind fully engaged. I grew to understand that was not his need. My thoughts were rude, unwelcome interruptions to the flow of his musings. What he wanted was to talk. And all he needed from me was my ears. If I could detach them from my head and set them on the table, I could walk away. So most times I sat nodding a lot, saying little. Walked up to the door deep breathed, prepared to play the bobblehead. Hand on handle. Turn it. Open slowly. And..."Hey Jon. Great practice son. How was your day?"

"Yeah. Fine." Puzzled. Where am I? Who is he? And where is my father?

I Am Jon

"Wanted to get your thoughts on a few things before the game tomorrow if you don't mind."

Huh? "Sure." I sat down at the table across from him cautious to say any more than I had planned before I came through the door.

"Jon, I think we really got a shot tomorrow. But I feel as though something is missing and I don't want to mess it up. You been on this team for almost as long as I have been coaching it. And if there is anybody that might know what it is, it is you." Stunned. Was this really happening? Between his vulnerability earlier and this, I really felt as though I had entered the twilight zone. Well if he really wanted my opinion, I was most certainly going to give it.

"Well dad, to be honest, I think there are two major things missing. They've been missing for quite a while now." I had his attention, and now that I did, I was going to say things I had always wanted to say. Things that always go stuck in my throat every time opened my mouth to voice them. "First, I think that God has been missing." Talk about starting with the bomb.

"God? What does God have to do with a basketball game?"

"Basketball? Maybe nothing. Maybe everything. I remember the days when you talked about Him more. Days when you believed that every step you took was directed. When we both felt that way."

"That was a long time ago."

Whiplash

"Yeah. Maybe too long. I remember nights when you came into my room and prayed for me."

"You were so young." Dad recoiled.

"Yeah but I remember. You would come into my room when you thought I was sleeping and pray with your hand on my forehead. And you would end the prayer the same way every night. 'May his steps be ordered, his life surrendered.'"

"...and your plan be accomplished in him'. Didn't know you heard me."

"I waited up for you every night Dad. I would pretend to be asleep, but I was awake, and, in my mind, I repeated it with you every time you said it. 'May his steps be ordered; his life be surrendered, and your plan be accomplished in him.' Every night. Then it all stopped."

He was nodding. Guilt and grief started to lay their sandbags on already rounded shoulders. "Then this job."

"No Dad. Before that. Then mom died. We never ever talk about her. When she died everything changed. And the dad I knew, the one who played catch with me and wrestled and told jokes, he died too." It was silent. The only noise in the house was hot air rattling the broken vent. "After mom died this job became everything dad. It was her replacement. Things been like this for so long I almost forgot you. You know what made me remember? Dee. God sent him to remind me that my steps are ordered, my life was surrendered, and His plan will be accomplished in me."

"I regret the day he walked into the gym."

"Well then you are really not going to like what I say next dad. Because I believe him walking into our gym that day was set up by God. God wanted to remind you of who you were. You used to be funny. Life used to follow you into the room. Everyone wanted to be around you." I could tell that he was uncomfortable, shifting in his chair.

"You are right. That used to be me, but that guy died a long time ago, and he ain't coming back." He got up and to walk away from the table. But I followed. He had made the mistake and opened a door that had stayed closed for years. Now my foot was wedged in it, and I wasn't gonna let it close so easy.

"It does not have to be that way dad. You just needed to be inspired. We both needed a breath of fresh air. And Dee was it. He saved us. Now it's time for you to allow him to do what he was called to do and put him in the game."

"Who are you, and where is my son?"

"Still here. Just a slightly better version that's all."

He walked away and went down the short hall toward his bedroom door. "I'll think about it." Door closed. And with that the moment was over and I was left to wonder if anything I said made any sense to him.

Chapter 15

SENIOR NIGHT

Thursday, February 3. Final home game of the season. Final home game for me at Providence, ever. Can't believe its been four years. Definitely had not turned out the way I planned it. By now we were supposed to have at least 2 trophies. College programs were supposed to be breaking down my door. But the trophy case was still reduced to the home for wayward posters and curious art projects, cause there were no more trophies in the case than when I started. And the tough life of a walk on at Junior College awaited me, that was if I wanted to keep playing ball. Still wasn't sure.

Either way this was still my senior night. A night I would gladly share with Ben, the only other senior on the team. I had known this guy for what seemed to be my whole life. Passed countless balls to him in the post both here and in Twelve Points Park. It was an honor to walk on to that floor for the last time with him. I had watched so many other guys on their senior nights and wondered what they were thinking. Some laughers. Some criers. Some laughcriers. You could never tell who was going to be who. Tonight, I would finally know which one would be me.

"Nervous?" Could always trust Michal to try to plug the feelings.

"Not really. More excited than anything. Plus, the big game is not till next week. Fremont ain't all that great this year. Should be an easy win."

"Stop that."

"Stop what?"

"Stop everything you just did. None of it was good and I don't like it. Stop minimizing your opponent. Even teams with bad seasons can have a good night. Don't underestimate them. And don't you dare let this night just pass you up. This is important. I don't care if you win or lose next week, tonight we celebrate. You are only a senior once." Big picture. Sometimes I got tired of Michal correcting me. She was like a walking conscience. But she always saw the big picture so clear, when I could often get lost in the legos.

"As usual you are right. But do me a favor and let's not talk about losing right now ok?" Michal laughed a good one.

"Fair enough."

Throughout the day people kept coming up to me. Congratulating me. Guess this is how it feels to retire. Halfway party. Halfway funeral. I took Michal's advice and appreciated it all though, my mind making permanent note of every comment. Most meaningful was surprisingly Mrs. Smith. She made

Senior Night

her way to my class just to talk to me. "You've always represented us well Jon. I am so proud of who you are. You have been one of the greatest examples of what this school can produce. You are going to do great things in life young man. Just promise me to remember that who you are always trumps what you do." I never forgot.

Dad had set the start time at 7, a little later than normal. With all the talk around the town, he wanted to give people time to get there. Expected a pretty good crowd. I pulled the bench over to the window in the locker room that faced the parking lot. It was 6:30 and the parking lot was already a sea of red lights that spilled out to street. Energy with the guys was good. Think this was going to be a pretty good night. "Everybody in town is coming tonight huh?"

"Yup. Principle gonna like these numbers. How much do you want to bet that he finds a way to get on the mic and say something." Izzie said strutting around like a proud man in a suit.

"You know he will." And he did.

The guys wanted Ben and I to come out of the locker room last. Nothing strange about that. But Ben insisted on walking out before me. We huddled one last time in our locker room. Dad gave the same rah rah speech he had given before every game. Then he stopped mid-sentence. Weird.

"Guys, I just want to say thank you. Thanks for letting me be your coach. It's been a great ride. Y'all taught me so much. Now you know I don't play favorites, but this is a special night for me. Every dad dreams of coaching his son, of his son being his point guard, or quarterback, or whatever. I've had the opportunity to live that dream. Son, thank you for allowing me to live that dream. It meant everything to me." He called me son. Then he hugged me. His eyes glistened. My eyes felt moist. Neither of us could speak.

Dee took over. "Let's go get this win boys. Let's send both our seniors out with a bang."

I did come out last. Proud parents came out on the floor. Ben's mom. My dad. The principle did get to the mic. He gushed about the year and thanked both of us for 4 years of hard work, sticking in a shameful plug for money somewhere in between. Then we both got the letters for our jackets. Is the principal grabbing the mic again? This is too much.

"Jon, please step forward." Kind applause. Can you put the mic down and get out of the way? We got a game to play. "Jon I've known you since you were a little little boy." This feels like a pinch the cheeks moment. He better not pinch my cheeks. "We all watched you grow up right here in this gym. And we are all proud of you. Always knew that one day you would wear that providence jersey." Polite nod and smile. "But it is not just what you did on the court. It's who you are as a person off the court that makes us most proud and represents what Providence as a school is all about. Now unfortunately you never got to raise any banners here, but we couldn't let

Senior Night

you leave without at least raising one. So the school board, faculty and students got together and voted, and we have decided to start an annual award. It gives me pleasure to name you our first ever Mr. Providence." With that, a curtain I never noticed fell revealing a banner with my name 'Jon Jacobs Jr. Mr. Providence.' And finally all the congratulations during the day, the conversation with Mrs. Smith, they all made sense.

My dad is proud. Chest is high. His eyes are glistening again. I love my dad. And my eyes were a little more than moist.

There was still a game to play that night and, in the end, I was right. It was a blowout win. But so was Michal. The win almost didn't matter. It was what happened before the whistle blew that meant the world to me.

Once again Dee never left the bench. And again, no one would ever know it.

I Am Jon

#INTHEWORD

1 SAMUEL 17
24 *Whenever the Israelites saw the man, they all fled from him in great fear.*

26 *Who is this uncircumcised Philistine that he should defy the armies of the living God?"*

32 *David said to Saul, "Let no one lose heart on account of this Philistine; your servant will go and fight him."*

---

1 SAMUEL 17
42 *Goliath looked at David with disgust.*

44 *He said to David, "Come here, and I'll feed your body to the birds and wild animals."*

Chapter 16

THERE IS ONE

Thursday, February 10th. I slept walked thru the day. Heard very little. Remembered even less. Honestly, being at school was a complete waste. Couldn't think about a formula or geological formation. All of that passed me unnoticed. I lacked the ability to absorb it because I was saturated with thoughts of the game that night. This was everything. Win and we qualify for the State Championships for the first time in 11 years. Beat Coastal, and Providence Basketball would finally mean something.

At lunch I sat playing with my food. Michal was talking to me. "You didn't hear a word I said, did you?"

"Sorry. Just thinking about this win, that's all. We need this."

"And suppose that doesn't happen."

"I am not entertaining that thought right now. We will win. It is our time."

"Well there is absolutely nothing on paper says that is possible. The 6'7" and 6'8 giants they got in the center say it ain't possible. The 6'4" point guard you

I Am Jon

will have to guard says it ain't possible. The newspaper says it ain't possible. Look into the faces of your own players Jon. I dare you to look into their faces and ask them if they believe they can win. I guarantee you that you will come to the same conclusion as the newspaper. Not one man on your team believes they can win that game. Not one. So stop playing yourself."

"Thanks so much for your expert analysis Michal. I can always count on your unsolicited opinion. But basketball isn't played on paper Michal now is it? It ain't just about how tall a team is right?" I was agitated. Her tell-it-like-it-is mentality was not welcomed this day. What I needed was motivation. This was caution tape and flashing yellow lights. "I got a plan for them."

"I heard your plan Jon and it ain't gonna work. Listen when we talked all them months ago, that was just pretend. Neither of us thought Providence would make it this far. But this is for real now bro. Y'all had a good season. A real good season. Think you should just be grateful for that."

"I am not in the mood for some participation trophy speech Michal. Whose side are you on anyway? If you want to support them then go find a blue t-shirt and wear it." There was venom in my words. The anger in me still burned hot because of what they had done. But she was probably voicing the opinion of everyone in Dyer, except me.

"Listen I'm a realist," she said. "I'm gonna tell it like I see it, and what I said is what I see. But when the

There Is One

whistle blows, I'll be sitting where I always sit. Right behind your bench, like I always am, and you know that."

The bus ride over to Coastal was silent. The only noise was the squeaking of the seats in that old yellow school bus. The boys sat in seats staring out windows. Couldn't tell if it was focus or fear I saw on their faces. Often those two look exactly the same. What Michal had said was stuck in my brain. Did any of these guys really think we could win? The thought was so loud it echoed in my brain until it was distracting. If I was going to go to war with this team, I needed to know they believed. I got up from my seat and marched to the front of the bus bracing myself against the driver's seat. "Guys I need your attention." The sound of my voice shook them out of silent daze. "I need to ask each of you a question and I need your honest answer. No fluff. No wild hopes. Just a real answer." They nodded. "Do you really believe we are going to win this game?"

Silence. No one volunteered to speak. Some returned to looking out of the window. Dad turned around shocked that he had not heard an immediate and resounding yes. "Did you guys hear Jon? Do you believe we will win this game or not?" he said. Shrugging shudders and a few illegible sounds.

Izzie was the bold one to break the silence probably because he was sitting in the seat right in front of me. "I mean, I think we could. Like, it's possible."

"That's not what I asked. I asked will we win?"

Ben. "We'll do our best Jon."

"That's not what I asked either Ben." I was starting to get annoyed. "Do you believe we will win or not? I mean if you don't why even bother to play this game?" I went down the bus one by one. Eleven players. Not one could look me in the face and convince me that they believed we would win. "Wow!"

Dan stood up. "You asked me to be honest. So here is honest. I told y'all that I went down to watch them play this summer. They are phenomenal. Freaks. It ain't even fair. And those giants on the inside? They are scary. My goal tonight is to keep it close. If we do that, we did good."

Dee stood up. "That's ridiculous. Course we are gonna win this game. Are you kidding me? We are gonna smash those boys." I ran down to the back of the bus where he was sitting so fast, I almost fell flat on my face.

"Dee you really believe that?"

"Of course I do. Absolutely."

Dad chimed in, "How would you know? You have never even played in a game son. What do you know about winning?"

"I know what it's like to fight sir. I know what it's like to scrap and claw and get punched in the face and refuse to fall. I won't tap out. I will not run away. And I am not scared. Cause greater is He that is in me than he that is in the world.[8] I believe that. So I am not afraid of them coach. They should be afraid

---

8   1 John 4:4

There Is One

of me! And if you ever put me on the court coach, you will see why." Every goose bump on my skin was raised and every follicle of hair stood at attention. Michal was wrong. I might have been foolish, but I was not foolish alone.

"That's it. That's all I needed. I just needed to know there was one." I returned to my seat with hot fire in my belly.

INTO THE FIRE

We arrived. Our bus slowly rolled into the parking lot past the grand entrance declaring we were on enemy territory. Had to push through cars that almost seemed abandoned on the side of the driveway. More cars spilling into the street, overflow from an already filled parking lot. It was still a full hour and a half before game time. The host school usually reserved a spot for the bus of the visiting team as a matter of courtesy. There was no parking spot for us. The bus driver came to a jerky stop in front of the entrance. "You guys get out here. I'll have to park at a church down the street."

There was an awkward pause, nobody moved, almost as if they thought about just forfeiting the game and going home. I finally said, "We ain't gonna win the game sitting on this bus. Let's go boys. Off the bus."

We huddled together on the sidewalk in front of Saber Gymnasium. Through glass walls I could see into the lobby. Well to do people at the smoothie bar, sculptures of their heroes adorning their halls. The self-playing grand piano and palatial waterfall. All the unnecessary accents that murdered the real needs on our campus. I saw it all and it still angered me.

Dad spoke to the security guard in the crowded lobby. "Sir we are the Providence basketball team, here for the game."

"I know who you are." No expression.

"Can you show us how to get to the visitors' locker room?" Dad said.

"Through there." He was pointing to the door to the gym without even looking in its direction.

"Is there not a way into the locker room without going through the gym?"

"Yes."

"Ok could you show us how to go that way?"

"No."

"And why is that?"

"The door is locked."

"Well does anybody have a key?"

"Yes. I do."

"Well can you unlock the door then sir?"

"No!"

"And why would that be?"

"I don't want to. You can go through the gym." Smirk on his face.

Dad saw the conversation was going nowhere and led us to the gym door. Deep breath. As it

There Is One

swung open there was a deafening sound. The fans had been waiting in ambush trying to get to us even before we put on our uniforms. The announcer grabbed the mic and hushed them."Shhhhh. Well, well, well. What do we have here? Providence scum."

The crowd responded, "Boo."

"We heard that you think you can beat us. Is this the best that Providence has to offer? Puny rejects? You must not know who we are. Let's tell them who we are." Then with war like rhythmic tone he shouted, "We are Coastal!"

The crowd responded with like cry, "Coastal Giants!"

"We are Coastal!"

"Coastal Giants!"

"What do we eat?"

"We eat lions!"

"What do we eat?"

"We eat lions!"

The game announcer was feeding the frenzy with blood dripping meat and we had not even gotten to the locker room. We walked across the court single file to the safety of the locker room door on the other side. Once in, we each found a place to sit everyone staring at the walls. The silence in the room was deafening, defeating. The fire I had found on the bus was reduced to a flicker by fear. Coach stood up, "I have never seen anything like that before. That was very unsportsmanlike. Downright evil. Felt like we were Hebrew boys in the fire didn't it?" I think he might have meant it as a joke. No one was laughing. "Boys we are here to do something great. Something that has never been done before. I don't know about you, but I did not expect it to come easy. Great victory always comes through great challenge. But we are up to this."

With that he called out the starting lineup. "Ben in the middle. Izzie, Dan, you got the three and the four. Jon at point. And...Dee you're in at the two. Now son I am taking a big risk on the biggest stage. But someone on this team said I needed to allow you to do what you do. So whatever that is, go do it. Plus I need someone out there who is foolish enough to think we can actually win tonight." Dee's smile was as wide as the horizon. So was mine. "Hands in. Let's go."

We came onto the court to greater ferocity than we had walked through just 30 minutes earlier. The gym was way past capacity. In the corners near our basket there were so many people standing that there was no visible sideline. The Providence fans that decided to brave the hurled insults, sat right behind our bench. Michal and Caleb were among them.

Warm up. Stretch. Layup drill. Free throws. Back to the bench. They introduced their team to flashing lights and smoke machines. They were as big as Dan had described. Giants in our eyes. We stood there thinking that they would introduce us. They never did. Another slight. Coach called us into a huddle. It

There Is One

was so loud I had to read his lips, "Guys we knew what to expect when we came here. None of this is new. So stay focused on the goal and don't get distracted by the noise!"

The five walked onto the center of the court and circled close so we could hear each other. Dee spoke first. "I know this is about to be TMI but I'm so nervous I almost released all my fluids. Just needed someone to know." Disgusted stare holding back the laughter. "By the looks of things you are as nervous as I am. You know what I do when I'm nervous? I pray. So I'm gonna pray right now." Dee bowed his head and prayed with such passion I got goose bumps even though I could hardly hear it all.

I jumped in. "Amen. Well since we are all sharing some TMI, let me share mine. You know what I do when I feel nervous before a game? I sing 'We Are The Champions' by Queen." They all gave me the disgusted, 'you cannot be serious' look.

"Jon you've got to be joking."

"No joke Izzie." Pointing to the bleachers I said, "What they want us to believe is that we are a losers and we don't belong on this court. But when I sing that song, I tell all those negative self-defeating thoughts, that I know who I am. I am a champion. God made me that way. And champions fight."

"We should sing it," Dee said overly excited.

"I promise you it will wipe the nervous willies away," I said. "Listen, I'll start it, y'all join in. And don't you leave me hanging."

We got to our tipoff positions. Ref grabbed the ball and headed to the center circle. The room was at the boiling point. I looked at them and started singing, "We are the champions my friend." It was so silly. So foolish. Knew they couldn't hear me, but they didn't have to. Dee joined in, "And we'll keep on fighting till the end." Before I knew it all five guys were howling heads thrown back, "We are the champions. We are the champions. No time for losers. Cause we are the champions of the world."

"Did Providence forget to send the basketball team and send the choir instead?" the announcer quipped. The crowd jeered. I didn't care. It looked silly to them, but it was freeing for us. And it was also distracting enough to the Coastal players that Ben got us the tip off.

"Boys, we just sang the Giants to sleep," Dee said with the loudest smile. The game had begun.

The Game

1 SAMUEL 17

45 *You come at me with sword and spear and battle-ax. I come at you in the name of God-of-the-Angel-Armies, the God of Israel's troops, whom you curse and mock. This very day God is handing you over to me.*

48-49 *That roused the Philistine, and he started toward David. David took off from the front line, running toward the Philistine. David reached into his pocket for a stone, slung it, and hit the Philistine hard in the forehead, embedding the stone deeply.*
The Philistine crashed, facedown in the dirt.

1 SAMUEL 31

11-13 *The people of Jabesh Gilead heard what the Philistines had done to Saul. Their valiant men sprang into action. They traveled all night, took the corpses of Saul and his three sons from the wall at Beth Shan, and carried them back to Jabesh*

Chapter 17

THE GAME

Great start but we were not the only ones with plans. They kept pounding it inside to their strength for ferocious tomahawk dunks. "All day! All day!" the tallest of the two said. They did that again, and again, and again. Every dunk harder than the one before. Don't think they took one jump shot in the first 5 minutes. The intention? Humiliate us into early submission. Evaporate any courage we had right at the beginning of the game.

But I was not about to let our courage crumble. "It's just two points boys. No matter how hard they dunk, no matter how loud they scream, it's only two points. Stay focused." And we did. We played ugly, gritty basketball and swiped and clawed our way to a few baskets and surviving their first wave. Quarter over. Score 15-8.

Second quarter began much the same way. They tried to pound it inside, but dad said, "Pack the paint. Make them shoot." So dunks became jumpers. Missed jumpers turned into rebounds. Ben was snatching rebounds like the last cookie from the

The Game

cookie jar. Outlet to Dee. Bounce pass to me. "Shoot that rock Jon," he yelled. Seemed like every time I did, I scored. "They can't stop you Jon. Shoot first apologize later." That happened a few times before I realized that I was on a roll. This is Newport again. It was going to be a good night for me. Score. 21-17.

Timeout Coastal.

The roar of the gym became an annoyed murmur. A 'what's going on' whisper. I could hear their coach tearing into them. He wasn't happy. "This team only has one player. One guy. Stop him."

Dad brought our attention back our huddle. "They didn't expect this boys. They thought this was going to be a cakewalk. Keep doing what you are doing, and don't you dare change a thing. Dig deep. They won't stop. Neither will you."

First play out of the timeout brought the same results. No room in the paint leading to a missed shot. I'm hearing some boos. Also hearing the spattering of brave Providence fans. Michal is on her feet leading the cheer. I can't believe it. This is amazing.

The next time we had the ball, I heard their coach call a defensive play, "kill, kill." The paint opened as wide as the ocean. "That's weird. But I'm taking it. I'm going straight to the basket." But as quickly as it opened it closed and the two giants converged on me. Their coach once again screamed, "kill, kill." And with that one of their players undercut me while the other absolutely crushed me with his shoulder.

I Am Jon

I think I heard a whistle. Not sure. I think that was intentional. I gotta get up and shoot these free throws. Man my leg really hurts. No big deal. I play against grown men in the park and hit the asphalt all the time. This is nothing. I'm gonna get up like I've gotten up every other time. Wait teammates aren't coming over. Why is no one coming over here? Is Ben crying? Why are the people in bleachers so silent? I'm starting to feel pain. Wow that's a lot of pain!

Dad came running over. "Did you hear a pop? Did you hear a pop son?" Reality hit. I couldn't even answer with words. Tears spoke for me because I had heard a pop and it drowned out the combined sound of the entire crowd in that gym. It was the sound of the end of seasons and dreams and hopes for me, and for him. The gym was respectfully silent as if witnessing the burial of a fallen soldier. Four men pushed passed the players and picked me up off of the floor. There was some applause from the crowd. Not much.

The whole team was in shock. When play restarted Coastal mercilessly took every advantage seeing we were wounded prey. Halftime. Score 35-21.

We literally limped into the half. By the time the other players made it to the locker room we all knew what had happened to me. Trainer confirmed that I tore my achilles. I could see it shriveled up the back of my leg. Every player came up to me to ask me how I was doing. Michal and Caleb came to see me as well. Felt like a body in a casket. Dad was withdrawn, head in hand. Had little to say.

The Game

Dan could not hold back his emotion. "That was intentional! They meant to hurt you."

Ben was still crying. Izzie was plotting payback.

Simon looked lost. He kept muttering to himself, "What are we supposed to do now?"

I was injured but I was still the leader of the team. A torn achilles could never take that away from me. "What do you mean, 'What are we going to do?' I am not dead, and this is not a funeral. We got a game to go win."

"How are we going to do that without you Jon? Who is going to score? Who is going to lead us?" Dan was only saying what others thought.

"I will." Dee said standing to his feet.

Ben exploded, "Stop it Dee! This not a joke man. Did you see what those boys did to Jon. They will do that to you too."

Dee shouted back, "You be afraid if you want Ben, but I am not afraid of them." He walked over to me and looked me in the eye. "Jon if you will be me on the bench, I will be you on the court." There was a confidence in his eyes. Like he had seen the end of the story or something.

"I got you. Bench covered. Now you go out there and do what we both know you were born to do. Go beat Coastal." Then I turned to the team. "I believe in Dee. I know that he can do this. I've always known he's more than capable of replacing me. Now all we need is you. Y'all want to make me feel better? Huh?" I pointed to my leg, "You want to make this worth it? Go out there and give me your best on that court. We don't cower down to cheats and cheap shots. We are Providence Lions. Since I am supposed to be Dee, it's my job to holler on the bench. And I promise you I'm about to holler. Now let's get out there and show these Giants how Lions roar." A spirit of defiance took over. There was a unified shout, a shift in the locker room. "Now we need one of those chant things that Dee does. But since I am Dee now, I guess that's my job. So repeat after me boys. We still believe!"

"We still believe!"
"We still believe!"
"We still believe!"
"We still believe!"
"We will win."
"AHHHHHHHHH!"

THIS IS IT

The boys asked me if I would to lead them out of the locker room and also asked Caleb if he would join us on the bench. Was my honor to lead this squad to the floor and take one last walk with my dad. Found an abandoned crutch in the corner of the locker room and I was good to go. Lined up at the door standing next to dad. He looked me in the face, "Jon I'm so proud to be your dad."

A world of emotions came over me. That was really all I ever wanted, for him to be proud of me. "No dad.

The Game

I'm the one who should be proud. I got to be your son. Now let's go to battle one last time."

We walked out of that locker room arm in arm, soldiers. To us, the crowd had once again disappeared, and the noise was silenced. All the newspaper articles and the history were forgotten. First half was erased. We huddled. Dad looked every player in the eye. "No more second fiddle to these guys. That comes to an end tonight. Believe in yourselves. Believe in us. Tonight we will battle. Tonight we will win."

Before Dee left the bench, I grabbed his hand. "Dee, be yourself. Your unconventional fearless self. Remember friend, being you has always been more than enough."

"Thanks Jon. But you don't have to worry about me. I don't know how to be anybody else."

Second half . The guy Dee was guarding got the ball. "Had no idea they let runts play high school ball."

Dee shot back unfazed, "Funny I had no idea babies played point guard. All you ever do is dribble."

"I'm gonna eat you for lunch." he said.

"Well this lunch is about to give you a terrible belly ache." Right then Dee swiped the ball from his hands, ran down the court with blinding speed. Layup. Score. "Eat that!" he said running back on defense rubbing his belly.

Dee was in his head now. "Who are you anyway. I don't even know your name."

"Just call me Jack. I'm a giant slayer!" Dribble. Dribble. Step back. Three. Score. 38-28.

Dee was doing his job. Was time for me to do mine, my best Dee impression. I jumped to my feet forgetting the achilles. "Ouch! Let's go boys! Let's go!"

"Dan lock him up son. Handcuffs baby."

Izzie hit a shot from just beyond the free throw line. "Make it rain Izzie. Make it rain."

We were diving to the floor. Jumping into crowds "Give me everything you got boys. Give me everything!"

Two on one fast break. Dee runs right at their center. He's back peddling. His legs are wobbling. Crossover. Around the back. Reverse layup. Blocking foul and the bucket. So pretty. The Providence fans erupted. End of quarter. 46-41. "Keep it up boys. They don't know what's hitting them."

Coastal was desperate to regain momentum. First play, they went back to what had worked early in the game. Toss the ball into the bigs and back up. Ben was guarding him. He backed Ben up under the rim and exploded for a one-handed dunk, leaving Ben on his back posterized. The gym was delirious. We had to take a timeout.

"S-s-sorry guys. I just can't guard him. H-he's t-t-too big." Ben looked to the floor as if he had let us down.

Dee was having none of that. "Stop that Benny. What does mom always say to us when we face a big challenge bro."

The Game

"If God is for us who can be against us."[9]

"Is God for us Benny? Is He for us?"

"Yea bro."

"Well then that big dude don't got a chance. Next time he tries to bully you in the paint use your smarts and let him know."

Score 58-56. 4 minutes to go.

For the next few minutes we went back and forth. What a battle. Dee hit a driving layup. Fouled. Made the free throw. We were down by one. The game was so intense that I bit off all my nails and had lost my voice.

Coastal went back to what worked. Big dude inside on Ben. "Smart Benny. Smart." He heard us. And just when Coastal's center lowered his shoulder to crash into Ben, he moved out of the way. The big dude lost his balance and lost the ball. Dee scooped it up and was sprinting down the court for a fast break layup.

Game tied. 45 seconds to go. Score 64-64.

Ben was jumping in the air, pumping his fist. Michal was standing on her seat. Dad threw his clip board. The rest of us were going nuts. Every breathing person with a voice left was shouting. Everyone on their feet. My heart was pounding so hard I could see my shirt shake. This was literally the best game I had ever seen. The size of the moment was getting to Coastal players too. Pressure will always reveal character, and it was sure revealing theirs. They were

---

[9] Romans 8:31

confused, barking each other. With all that chaos, their point guard came down the court and threw the ball out of bounds.

Providence ball 28 seconds to go.

Dad was about to call a time out. I stopped him. "Leave it alone. No plays. No interruptions. Just give the ball to Dee." Strange look. Then he called it.

"Dee's ball. Iso. Clear out." 18 seconds to go

Dee got the ball at the top of the key, one eye on the defender the other on the clock. Dribble, dribble. "What is he doing. The clock is gonna run out."

"Just watch. I believe."

12 seconds. Dribble, dribble.

The clock hit 10 seconds and Dee made a quick move and bolted for the key. The giants are ahead of him, his defender was on his back and there is no time to change his mind. Floater, just above the outstretched hands of the approaching wall. Bodies crash into each other. Ball rolls on the rim. Round and round. And then goes through the net. Hands on heads. Hands in the air. The game is over. Providence wins. Providence wins. I'm hugging dad. He's hugging me. Everyone mobbed Dee. We did it. We slew the giants.

"Dee screamed, "We believe."

"We believe."

"We believe."

"We believe."

The Game

UNFINISHED BUSINESS

The local newspaper reporter made his way into the scrum and dug Dee out of it. "Son what is your name? I didn't even know you were on the roster. Where have you been all season?"

"Oh, pumping balls, sweeping floors and waiting my turn."

That reporter spent all his time interviewing Dee never once thinking to talk to me…or to dad. After all those years of losing, no one recognized him when we finally won.

"What does it feel like to finally lead Providence to the State playoffs? You are a star now."

But Dee was not about to drink that Kool-Aid. The guy that I knew in the dark, when he wore the managers jacket and held a broom, was the same guy in the light. He used his newfound light to shine on others.

"With all due respect, this was not about me sir. Not at all. We are a team, and every guy on the court and on the bench was a part of this. But more than any of us, this was about God. He did this. This win belongs to Him!"

After about 5 minutes Dee said' "Excuse me sir. I have something important to attend to." He came over to where I was and said, "Jon we got some unfinished business. Let's go."

I Am Jon

With that Dee led the entire team to the Coastal locker room door and opened it. He pushed past the guy at the entrance and walked into the heart of the locker room where their team was still sitting dejected.

When they saw us the entire team stood up. They were not standing to welcome us. The talker that guarded Dee said, "What are you doing in here? What do you want?"

"Good game. We didn't get a chance to congratulate you, so we came to shake yours."

"We are not interested in shaking your hands."

"Ok then. That's up to you. But we also came in here to retrieve something that belongs to us."

With that, Dee walked up to the wall where the defamed poster of dad and I was hanging torn. He took it down, rolled it up, and gave it to me.

EPILOGUE

We did end up going to the state championships. We lost in the first round, but it was an amazing experience. A small team from the little town of Dyer. But people knew us now. We were the team that beat the Giants.

That state playoff game was the last one dad would coach. Decided that he did not have the heart for it anymore. Two years later he retired from teaching all together and returned to his first love, under the hoods of cars at Pop's shop. He never really talked about coaching again. In his post basketball years Dad and I talked often. I was reintroduced to the man I had known. The one even he thought had died. Those were precious years to me. Dad died after a 10 year battle with cancer. But we had said all that we needed to. I was at peace.

Dee had an amazing career at Dyer. Two years later he returned the program to State playoffs and they won the whole thing. Dee was recruited by a few big-time schools but chose to play for State. After college Dee went on to play a few years in some professional league overseas before returning to Dyer.

I Am Jon

And me? That Coastal game was the last one I would ever play. The injury helped me realize that it was never so much that I loved the game of basketball, as much as I loved my dad. And when he stepped away, I decided it was a good time for me to step away too. But my time at Providence did introduce me to my first love. Teaching. So I left Dyer and went across country to study and I became a math teacher. When I was finished with school I settled there in the big city and thought about that little sleepy town very little.

Sometime later I received a curious letter. It was from Providednce High. They renovated that old gym, finally, and wanted me to come back for the opening ceremony. They were going to be honoring my dad. Many of the old players were going to be there. Izzie, Ash, Dan, Simon, Caleb and Ben.

On that day I sat in the audience listening to all these people talk about my dad, coach Jon Jacobs. It was so great to see the boys again after so many years.

But the one moment, more than any, that meant everything to me came later. Seated on stage was my old friend, the new coach of the Providence Lion's, Dee. And in the front row? His wife Michal.

He got up and started his speech. "Let me tell you how I ended up on one of the greatest basketball teams ever. Started with a visit to a gym, pumping some balls and a friend who saw greatness in me."

Epilogue

He continued, "It was an honor to play for that man. And so it gives me pleasure to announce the renaming of the Providence Gym, the John R Jacobs Gymnasium." I was so proud.

Some people have asked if I ever resented Dee. They say it seems as though he stole the good life that was meant for me. But I harbor no resentment against him at all, only love, and gratitude.

Love, because he was truly my friend. More than a brother. Gratitude because, looking back, I can see that he was the tool God used to pry me free from the dreams that others had for me, dreams that I would never fit, and introduce me to the purpose He always had planned. For when the door to Dad's dream for me finally closed, the door to God's dream for my life swung wide open.

JEREMIAH 29:11
I know what I'm doing. I have it all planned out—plans to take care of you, not abandon you, plans to give you the future you hope for.

ABOUT THE AUTHOR

DAMIAN CHANDLER is a pastor and story teller who has served congregations from Seattle Washington to Huntsville Alabama. He is currently the senior pastor of the Capitol City Seventh-day Adventist Church in sunny Sacramento California. He is also the author of the Amazon Best Seller, The Crooked Christmas Tree. He gets to share life with his wife Tanzy and their three children Zoe, Salem and Levi.

www.ingramcontent.com/pod-product-compliance
Lightning Source LLC
Chambersburg PA
CBHW062033120526
44592CB00036B/1991